# TOP SECRET ULTRA

# TOP SECRET ULTRA

## PETER CALVOCORESSI

PANTHEON BOOKS
NEW YORK

LIBRARY OF CONGRESS CATALOGING IN PUBLICATION DATA

Calvocoressi, Peter.
Top secret ultra.

1. World War, 1939-1945—Cryptography.
2. World War, 1939-1945—Secret service—Great
Britain. 3. World War, 1939-1945—Personal
narratives. English. 4. Calvocoressi, Peter.
I. Title.
D810.c88c34      940.54'86'41      80-7708
ISBN 0-394-51154-9

Manufactured in the United States of America

FIRST AMERICAN EDITION

# CONTENTS

# ILLUSTRATIONS

# FOREWORD

This is a book about one aspect of intelligence during the second World War: the breaking of German high-grade cyphers and the operational and strategic uses of these breaks. The flood of intelligence from this source was huge and unexpected. Its subject matter was at first scrappy, puzzling and unfamiliar; but it was mastered. Its dissemination to commanders in battle was unforeseen; but it became an expert routine. I have tried here to make an assessment of its impact on the way the war went. The historian's problem is not to judge whether Ultra was crucial to victory or merely peripheral but to show where it was the one and where the other: for it was both.

This is not a history of intelligence, still less another history of the war. It is an attempt to evaluate a single but extraordinary source.

I have mentioned few names in this book because, in writing it, I have had in mind not my own generation who may like to be reminded of one another, but younger generations for whom our names do not matter.

This is a short book because I have stuck to what I know and remember; and because, as Leonard Woolf used to say, there never was a book which could not be improved by cutting.

Aspley Guise
August 1979

PJAC

# 1 BLETCHLEY PARK

Bletchley Park is a house of medium size in modest grounds some fifty miles north-west of London. It was bought by the British government between the wars to house its Codes and Cyphers School and was occupied by this organization when war broke out in September 1939. BP, as it was familiarly called, was more remarkable for its human complement than its architectural dignity. The house had been built shortly before or shortly after the end of the nineteenth century in a style which, up to a few years ago, has been adjudged ridiculous. Even from the more generous or quizzical standpoint of today it is not a striking example of the taste of its times and inside it was dreadful. I remember a lot of heavy wooden panelling enlivened here and there by Alhambresque (Leicester Square, not Granada, Andalusia) decorative fancies. There was a modest stable block and grounds of a few acres laid out as a small park rather than gardens. In a pond in front of the house a few ducks had survived the transfer of the property to government ownership.

Here, during the war, worked thousands of men and women. They were all concerned either with the breaking of codes and cyphers of various grades and in numerous languages, or in appraising and passing on the intelligence won from these breaks. This book is about a part only of all this work — namely, the breaking of the German high-grade wireless traffic encyphered on the Enigma machine, and the handling and uses of the resulting intelligence, which we called Ultra.

Enigma was the name given by the Germans to their machine. Ultra was the name given by us to the intelligence we got from breaking Enigma. Top Secret Ultra, to give it its full name, was a grade or category of intelligence. It applied to documents and to what was in them. Some things were Secret, others were Most Secret. But Most Secret did not mean what it said. For some things were more secret than Most Secret. These were Most Secret Ultra — changed to the dubiously grammatical Top Secret Ultra when the Americans came into the war.

3

The breaking of Enigma cyphers played a significant part in the second World War. The value of its contribution varied from time to time and from theatre to theatre, but from the middle of 1940 it was an ever-present factor. To say that it won the war or even that it won a particular battle would be a silly exaggeration as well as a gross oversimplification of how wars and battles go. But without doubt Ultra made a big difference, sometimes a vital one.

All intelligence provides valuable background information but the Ultra intelligence which came from breaking Enigma cyphers did far more than that. It could sway battles and save lives, and it gave staffs and commanders an unparalleled insight into enemy dispositions, capabilities and intentions.

The importance of intelligence about the enemy is obvious. To know his strength, his order of battle, his mind — all this is crucial, particularly when he is stronger and winning. There are many ways of getting this information. Most of them involve either intermediaries such as spies of varying dependability, or guessing based on varying degrees of insight. But one method is in a class by itself. This is overhearing what the enemy himself is reporting to himself about himself. A primitive form of this class of intelligence is stealing secret documents from filing cabinets or waste-paper baskets, and this still goes on. But it is usually a slow as well as a chancy business and it involves recruiting an adequately talented and reliable thief or suborning a traitor.

Ultra intelligence had none of these drawbacks and it did have two enormous advantages. The most useful intelligence needs to be both authentic and prompt. Ultra was authentic because it consisted of overheard talk between German commanders themselves. And it could be unbeatably prompt. In the nature of things a wireless message is intercepted the instant it is transmitted. It is not so easily or immediately decyphered but, given successful cryptographers, it may be read with almost equal celerity. This did not happen all the time or with all high-grade cyphers (some of which we never read at all), but we did become used to reading regularly a great many messages between one German unit and another within hours of the time when they were put on the air.

There is even a case where we seem to have read a German directive before it was read by its legitimate recipient. Field

Marshal Kesselring, who was Commander-in-Chief of all German forces in the Mediterranean theatre, sent certain instructions to Rommel in North Africa. Rommel's headquarters received Kesselring's message but signalled back that it was corrupt and could not be understood: please repeat. Meanwhile the original message had been intercepted and decyphered in England and its gist relayed to Montgomery who was reading his version at about the time when the repeat from Kesselring lay before Rommel. This is an extreme and rare example but not an impossible one. It has, however, a twist to it. Rommel's request for a repeat may have been made not because he could not understand the original but because he did not like what he read and wanted to do his own thing before being told not to: calling for a repeat was perhaps simply delaying tactics. But as an example of what Ultra might do the story may stand.

Two inventions lay behind these activities: the petrol engine and radio. As soon as men began to go to war in mechanized vehicles, whether on the ground or in the air, they created for themselves a problem in communications. They moved rapidly away from their bases and from each other. Not only could they no longer wave flags at each other; they could not rely on the telephone system which was likely to be unfamiliar (because in a foreign country), partially destroyed, in the wrong places, and insecure. Radio provided remedies for all these defects except the last. It enabled a commander to communicate with his superiors, his fellows and his base, from wherever he might happen to land up. The only trouble was that wireless telegraphy was like a loud-hailer. It could be used to shout to your friend but it was impossible to be sure that your enemy could not hear what you were saying.

Sometimes it did not matter. Sometimes the urgency was such that the risk was worth taking. But for a vast amount of information or orders secrecy was essential, and this was achieved by cyphering.

A cypher is simply a way of making nonsense of a text to everybody who does not have a key to it. The sender jumbles his text but the recipient knows how he has done this and so can disentangle and restore the original words. Cryptography is the search for the key by the man who has not got it and is not supposed to have it.

5

Cyphers range from the simplest transposition which achieves little beyond delaying the laying bare of the text, to the most complex processes which produce something that is virtually undecypherable. The degree of complexity adopted depends on the importance of the traffic which that cypher is intended to carry. The more complicated cyphers require more time and equipment and above all their use needs to be restricted in order to minimize the opportunities for breaking them and the damage if they are broken. The introduction of machines to do the encyphering greatly extended the range of attainable complexity and therefore the problems of decyphering, for which machines had to be invented too.

The amount of Enigma traffic put into the air every day was colossal. I have found no way of measuring it but it certainly ran into those regions where figures become almost meaningless. What I can say is that, for the greater part of the war, this traffic was being systematically, regularly and extensively decyphered and that by 1944, out of the mass of information obtained in this way, enough was of sufficient operational importance to require intelligence officers handling it at BP to signal it to British and American commanders in the field at the rate of about 5 signals per hour round the clock (excluding naval traffic which, as we shall see, was handled separately). And this was only a selection. The aggregate amount of Ultra intelligence about the German war effort stored in our brains and card indexes but not signalled to commands overseas was perhaps ten or twenty times as bulky as that.[1]

My purpose in this book is to explain how this was done and to assess the consequences. It is written from the viewpoint of somebody who was at Bletchley Park and I shall begin by describing the rather curious way I got there. There is historical interest in recording who we were as well as what we did there.

When the war started I was a very unlikely candidate for Secret Intelligence. Although a British subject by birth owing to the accident of my having been born in India I was and am

[1] The precise number of non-naval signals sent to commands between 18 November 1943 and 15 May 1945 was 52, 084. Signals sent before 18 November 1943 had not reached the PRO when I finished writing this book. This total excludes a small number of signals sent with a specially restricted circulation: see Appendix One, paragraph 2.

entirely Greek. My father, by an analogous accident, had been born a French citizen and had been brought up in Constantinople. He became a naturalized British subject during the first World War or soon after it but when I had wanted to join the diplomatic service after leaving Oxford in 1934 I was not acceptable. The rules said that a candidate had to be a British subject by birth, which I was, and the son of British-born parents, which I was not. How much less likely that I should ever be allowed into secret intelligence work. Not that I ever gave it a moment's thought, up to the very day when I found myself doing Ultra secret work.

Yet I was an insider as well as an outsider. I belonged to a community which was in most respects self-sufficient, but not in all. This was the close and prosperous inner community of Chiots which existed within the wider community of Greeks in London, Liverpool, Manchester and other such places. We were the descendants of those who had escaped westward at the time of the famous massacre on the island of Chios in 1822 (depicted by Delacroix and hymned by Victor Hugo). These Chiots founded their own businesses and intermarried. Socially and professionally they lived their own lives, looking to one another for most of the goods and comforts needed between cradle and grave, including in particular jobs and spouses. But one thing they could not provide: education. So boys like myself were despatched into the English educational system. I went in more than half Greek and came out more than half English. This was a second migration. The first was geographical and forced on the Chiots by the massacre. The second was cultural, less forcible but ultimately no less fateful.

The education I received was excellent. Also, although I did not realize this at the time, it gave me a passport. Having emerged from Eton and Balliol I had become, potentially at least, Establishment material. I had also picked up a couple of secondary advantages in academic distinction (a scholarship at Eton and a First at Oxford) and a facility for languages. In the ordinary course of events I might be a somewhat disadvantaged member of the Establishment, endowed with a tongue-twisting name and debarred from some kinds of official employment. But given a crisis the system would be flexible enough or desperate enough to take me right in.

In the autumn of 1939, 26 years old and recently married, I

7

had even less wish than most people to rush off and risk my life. I was content to evade the conflict between family happiness and a wider duty by accepting the current orthodoxy which said that one should wait one's turn to be called up in an orderly manner and when required. I had been called to the Bar in 1935 and along with a number of other barristers I was temporarily recruited into the Ministry of Economic Warfare which was established in the London School of Economics off Aldwych in London. Its job was to find the bottlenecks in the German economy and squeeze them. Some optimists thought that in this way the German war machine could be brought to a halt by Christmas but this euphoria did not survive the test of experience and the Ministry, having been shifted to more commodious quarters in Berkeley Square, settled to a less spectacular but none the less useful role in the war.

Meanwhile my personal contribution began to seem shamefully jejune and when the phoney war was succeeded by disasters in the west in the spring of 1940 I decided I ought to do something more active than impede the neutrals' commerce with Germany. I resolved to volunteer for the army instead of waiting to be called up. There was some calculation in this decision since, if I remember right, a volunteer might be commissioned straight away whereas a conscript would not be able to avoid the presumed discomforts of 'the ranks'. Which of these two motives weighed more with me I would not at this distance of time like to say. Combined they led me to the War Office.

There I spent the best part of a day shunting from room to room, answering questions and undergoing tests. At the end of it all I arrived in an office where the accumulated results of the day's experiences lay tabulated on a sheet of paper with, at the foot, a verdict. Although from where I sat it was upside down, I could read it clearly enough. It ran: 'No good, not even for intelligence.'

This, as it seemed to me, overemphatic verdict derived from the fact that a few years earlier I had cracked my head in a motor accident. I returned to the Ministry to relate this humiliating outcome to my colleagues. One of them said: 'Why not try the Air Ministry? My father is the Director of Intelligence there.'[1] I wrote at once. A week later I had an interview — not

[1] There was no unified Ministry of Defence in those days. Navy, army and air force pursued their autonomous existences in their

8

with the Director of Intelligence who, I am sure, never heard of me — and a week after that a commission.

The RAF was desperate for intelligence officers (it had only two or three dozen all told at the outbreak of war) and since I was ruled unfit for flying duties because of my accident I was snapped up. The Directorate of Intelligence had taken on somebody from the Portuguese wine trade and given him an office round the corner from the Ritz with instructions to cast a wide net for reasonably suitable 'officer material'. I spent a number of months on fighter stations in the north of England and I had just been transferred to the HQ of Fighter Command at Stanmore near London when one day I was summoned to a part of the Air Ministry which was lodged in a sub-basement of a recently erected concrete block near Lambeth Bridge. Even the interviewer looked sinister, though later I discovered he was nothing worse than an academic psychologist roped into intelligence rather like myself. With the minimum of words he handed me a piece of paper and asked me to translate what I saw there. It was in German, which I expected, and was all about parachuting, which I did not. As I translated I reached the logical conclusion that I was destined to be parachuted into an area where fluent German would be required, and I faced this unalluring prospect with the sangfroid inculcated by my English education.

But I was now directed to another gloomy building which was in fact the HQ of the so-called Secret Service in Broadway, near St James's Park. At this place, more dingy than sinister, I went up in one of those lifts that move with a slow clatter and along corridors that are painted dark brown from the floor up to about four feet. This was the prelude to my first and, until 1977, last meeting with Group Captain Fred Winterbotham, of whom at that time I had very properly never heard. Winterbotham told me that I had been chosen for specially secret work, so secret that my name would be on a list which had to be submitted to Churchill. I was then given a one-way ticket to Bletchley, a small town which had grown round a railway junction 50 miles north-west of London and half way between Oxford and Cambridge.

separate Whitehall departments of the Admiralty, War Office and Air Ministry. Even their names seemed carefully chosen to avoid any suggestion that they had much in common.

What I found there astounded me. Here was an organization which was decyphering highly secret German wireless traffic every day. It had never crossed my mind that this sort of thing went on. I knew of the interception and decoding of the Zimmermann telegram in the first World War but such coups I thought of as no more than war's fancy frills. BP was not like that. It might be tucked away in the middle of England, miles from the front and from danger, but it was obviously no peripheral show. In its own way it was in the heart of things.

In some ways I was a fairly typical member of BP. Besides possessing certain basic qualifications such as knowledge of German I came from the right educational establishments and I belonged more rather than less to a world where people looking for recruits would look — a restricted middle-class professional world where it was comparatively easy to get trustworthy reports about individuals.

There were at BP Chiefs and Indians. The Chiefs in both areas — cryptography and intelligence — were distinguished from the Indians because they were fewer and preponderantly male and had the better jobs — better because they were more responsible and closer to the brush of real events. But the Chiefs were not a different kind of person in the way that, in the armed services, officers were officers and men were men. The reason for this lay in the nature of the work done by the Indians.

Both cryptography and intelligence rested upon the assembling, ordering and understanding of a great mass of superficially trivial or unilluminating snippets of raw material. In the case of cryptography, this raw material consisted of a flood of scraps of paper which were alike in being unintelligible because undecyphered, but separable in so far as they could be sorted into categories by reference to their frequencies or call signs. The first stage in the decyphering process was to sort this mass, in what was called the Registration Room, into piles of related material. This was where the first chinks of light were brought to illuminate the mass. Decyphering rested upon a series of winnowings leading to the isolation of a single message which could be made to yield the key to a whole run of messages.

In intelligence likewise the beginning of wisdom lay in categorizing and recording thousands of snippets of information which, although not unintelligible since they had been rendered into German and thence into English, were nevertheless largely pointless. By itself a message instructing X to go to Y is trivial. But in association with other trivialities it may become revealing. One may know X and know that he is an important man in a special field, so that his whereabouts are always a matter of interest; and one may be exceptionally concerned with whatever goes on at Y and whoever goes there. The fact that X has been sent to Y is never an isolated fact. It is simply one fact in an enemy world which intelligence is for ever striving to see more of. A large part of the business of intelligence was to be in possession of associated facts, recent or remote, and to be skilled in making the correct associations. (Example: a message about the movements of '65 Army Corps I G' is transformed if you know that this officer is Obersturmbannführer Dr Hoehne, the commander of the SS Wehrgeologen battalion which is engaged in the seismographic plotting of rocket missiles.)

In cryptographic and intelligence work the Indians had to have well-trained minds, a considerable knowledge of the subject matter with which they were dealing, their wits about them, and a measure of resourcefulness. So, like their Chiefs, most of them came from universities and had honours degrees.

The Chiefs formed two distinct groups. In the one, cryptography, the problems were essentially mathematical and so the cryptographers were mainly mathematicians with, in second place, a sprinkling of chess-players whose characteristic contribution was to think about what the opponents' next move but one might be. There were in 1939 two cryptographers working on Enigma — and in the opinion of some wasting their time — but others had been provisionally recruited and arrived at BP in September. As time went on and the needs grew further reinforcements were procured. They came from the mathematics departments at Cambridge and other universities but also, as we shall see, from less likely quarters.

On the intelligence side the one essential qualification was a thorough knowledge of German. University teachers and schoolmasters constituted the largest single group but I remember too a couple of curators from the British and the Victoria and Albert Museums, a business man or two, lawyers and writers. Like the cryptographers we in intelligence were all

11

civilians in pre-war days and young. Some of us wore uniforms as temporary members of one or other of the armed services but I remember only one regular officer in those parts of BP intelligence with which I was concerned. Most of us were between 25 and 30 when we went to BP. Some were older, a few younger still.

Of the service departments the Admiralty had been most alive, before the war, to the need to recruit civilians for wartime intelligence but none had foreseen how much that need would expand. Pre-war recruiting was on a modest scale. A few potential Chiefs had been marked down and approached. This was done quietly and privately. There was in the Admiralty a list of 'gentlemen who had offered their services to the Admiralty in the event of hostilities', and in the months before war began the Director of Naval Intelligence got an outsider — in fact the novelist Charles Morgan — to go through this list and pick out 40-50 of the more promising volunteers. Ian Fleming , creator of 007 James Bond, was one of them. All three services and the Foreign Office also made discreet inquiries of relatives and friends, tapping universities, public schools, the business world and similar potential reservoirs of talent and discretion. This process continued after war began but the reservoirs dried up with general mobilization.

Recruiters followed their noses, making personal inquiries in a manner more familiar to merchant bankers or wine merchants than to government service. They used the somewhat discredited but indubitably efficacious old-boy net. They made forays into schools and colleges, board rooms and clubs. They put questions that were veiled and yet understood. They could not say precisely what they were looking for, but between friends and over a glass of sherry enough would be conveyed: bright chaps for hush-hush jobs. Characteristically perhaps they underrated at first the possibilities of the old-girl net as distinct from the old-boy net, but this was quickly remedied under the pressures of necessity. One senior BP cryptographer, for example, had had a sister who had been a Fellow of Newnham College, Cambridge. He therefore knew a number of Fellows of that college and soon a posse of clever girls from Newnham arrived in his department.

Another feature of these forays which may be thought to be typical of the English educated middle class was the emphasis on quality rather than qualifications. At one famous public school the question put was: Who is the cleverest boy you have got here? The answer was that so-and-so was the cleverest boy but he would not do for what was presumed to be required because he was a classical scholar and no good at maths. But the search party thought otherwise and put its tabs on the classical scholar who became one of BP's outstanding cryptographers.

When I arrived at BP some time in 1941 or 1942 the grounds were dotted with huts which had been run up to cope with the staff explosion engendered by success. The house itself was too small for more than a handful of top brass and their immediate acolytes. These huts were wooden shacks. Hut 3, where I worked, was a narrow single-storey structure divided into rooms of different sizes on either side of a pokey longitudinal corridor. Hut 6 was another such hut. Soon after my arrival a more solid and draught-proof building was erected, brick rather than timber, and was shared by Huts 6 and 3. But we kept our separate names which were by then not so much addresses as descriptions of our functions. None of these buildings now exists — with one solitary exception. Near the house there remains a rather disconsolate wooden hut which was either the original Hut 3 or one of its twins.

The Ultra community at BP saw itself as — perhaps was — an élite within an élite. Many of the things which made it successful made it also intense: the narrow catchment area, the smallness (as I shall show) of its cryptographic and intelligence sections, the edgy pressures of relentless work round the clock, the sense of responsibility and achievement, and the fact that there was no escape. The rule, dictated by security, was: once in, never out. And this rule was rarely broken. There was a board or committee to which an inmate of BP might address a plea for a posting elsewhere. An application to this board would be followed by an interview and, almost invariably, the rejection of the plea. A girl who had broken her heart and wanted to get away to give it a chance to mend might find sympathy but she would not get release. The only transients on the Ultra side were officers who came to BP to be indoctrinated and trained before going to intelligence staffs in the field where they would handle Ultra material.

It is easier to recall the excellence of our collaboration in this

Ultra sub-community than to explain how it came about. There was of course the high seriousness of war. There was the fact that we were extremely busy and knew ourselves to be successful and our labours to be valuable. There was also another factor, one not altogether palatable. As a consequence of the recruitment that I have tried to describe, nearly all of us had had the same sort of education and shared a common social background. We made, unwittingly for the most part, the same assumptions about life and work and discipline and values. Although we had never met before — among several thousand people at BP there was only one, Henry Whitehead, whom I had known before the war (at Balliol, ten years earlier) — we half knew each other already. We fell easily into comradeship and collaboration. And these facts go some way to explain the astonishing further fact that the Ultra secret was kept not merely during the war but for thirty years afterwards — a phenomenon that may well be unparalleled in history.

But such personal considerations cannot by themselves account for BP's successes. There were institutional factors too.

Wartime BP evolved out of the Government Codes and Cyphers School, and GC&CS was originally what its name implied and no more. It was a cryptographic establishment which made up codes and cyphers for our own use and worked to break the codes and cyphers used by others. It was — this is the first important point about it — unique in the sense that it had in Britain no competitors. Furthermore it was converted from a purely cryptographic establishment into a full working partnership of cryptographers and intelligence. This comprehensiveness was a vastly important factor in its success.

The fact that it embraced all grades of cypher in all languages brought psychological and technical benefits. Psychologically this inclusiveness was valuable because the consequent concentration of talent was intellectually stimulating. Technically it is desirable to have a close association between cryptographers working on different grades because a message in a low-grade (and so easily breakable) cypher may be retransmitted, verbatim or with minor alterations, in a cypher of a higher grade, thus creating opportunities for breaking the latter, or vice versa. Such a re-transmission violates the basic rules of cypher security but it happens all the same: for example, weather reports transmitted by U-boats using Enigma were not infrequently re-transmitted verbatim in lower grade cyphers.

There is a peculiarly horrible example of the links between cyphers of different grades. The basic problem is cryptography is to get randomness. Left to themselves human beings, and machines operated by human beings, quickly stop being purely random and fall into some pattern or other. At one point the German cryptographers responsible for finding entirely random settings for an Enigma cypher thought that they had hit on a bright solution. Every day the concentration camps rendered returns giving the numbers of prisoners who had been delivered to the camp that day, the number who had died or been killed, and the number of surviving inmates at the end of the day. These were truly random figures. They were reported in a medium-grade cypher and the recipients passed them on to their Enigma colleagues who used them in determining the settings of a particular Enigma cypher. BP was reading that medium-grade cypher and it realized too that these daily concentration camp returns were being used in Enigma. So these sad, grisly statistics of human suffering and indignity played a part which the piteous victims never dreamed of.

BP was comprehensive in another way too. It was inter-service and non-service. This was much more remarkable in the thirties and forties than it may seem today. BP's direct ancestor was the celebrated Room 40 in the Admiralty which brought off a series of cryptographic coups in the first World War, including the reading of the Zimmermann telegram. But soon after the end of that war Room 40's activities were taken over by the Foreign Office. This switch had good and bad effects. It down-graded service intelligence (which was by the late thirties pathetically undernourished by comparison with political intelligence) but it also prepared the way for inter-service collaboration of a kind unparalleled elsewhere in the world. This collaboration was not achieved painlessly or even completely but by the time war came again in 1939 it was institutionalized, more cordial than, for example, in the USA, and immensely more effective than in Germany where six or seven different cryptographic establishments fought each other almost as venomously as they fought the enemy.

Finally, BP's comprehensiveness, was consummated when intelligence was grafted on to cryptography and these two partners were set to work in the same compound. Producers and consumers were cheek by jowl and the constant, easy and fruitful interchanges between the two — mostly by word of mouth, between people who saw one another every day — were a major element in their joint achievement.

At the same time there were divisions within BP. The very special nature of the Ultra source dictated some segregation on grounds of security. Only a minority of those at BP knew about Ultra. Furthermore, Ultra had its own lines of communication to clients in the outside world: the three service departments (navy, army and air) and the SIS in London, and commanders in the field. (The former were served by teleprinter and by bag and the latter by a special wireless network to which I shall return below). Ultra was to this extent kept apart and so therefore were those working on it.

There was another distinction, based on practical considerations. Naval Ultra was handled differently from the rest.

The War Office and the army's Imperial General Staff, the Air Ministry and Air Staff, did not conduct operations. The Admiralty and Naval Staff did. The Admiralty was an operational HQ as well as a department of state. The army and air staffs issued directives of a general nature. The Admiralty gave orders during a battle. Thus the Imperial General Staff might direct a Commander-in-Chief to clear the enemy out of, say, Africa. It would not tell him how to do it, nor would it intervene in the course of a battle except in very exceptional circumstances. On the other hand naval commanders, including admirals afloat, might get orders from London from day to day or even hour to hour. The First Sea Lord was like nobody else in the British war machine.

This distinction was mirrored in the organization at BP. Cryptographers and intelligence dealing with naval Enigma worked in Huts 8 and 4 (Naval Section) while the comparable work on other services — army and air and also the SS, police and railways — went on in Huts 6 and 3. The former served one master, the latter several. The former sent verbatim translations of naval decodes to London and nowhere else. The latter sent similar translations to London but also sent to commanders in various theatres of war signals based on selected

16

German messages, about which I shall have more to say later on in this book.

There was one exception to the rule about naval traffic. During the war in the Mediterranean the Admiralty allowed some naval intelligence (not as it happened Ultra intelligence) to be sent directly from BP to the theatre instead of being routed through the Admiralty. This was partly to save time but more because of the nature of the case. Intelligence about the supplying of the German and Italian armies in North Africa came from two principal sources — Italian naval cyphers giving information about sailings from Italian and Greek ports, and German Luftwaffe traffic on Enigma which gave details of air escorts and reconnaissance. The two sources had to be married in order to get the most advantage out of either. This was done at BP and the resulting intelligence was transmitted directly from BP to Commanders-in-Chief in the Mediterranean. This exception to the general rule demonstrates the flexibility of the British intelligence system

\*

I conclude this chapter with a brief survey of this intelligence world as it was when war broke out. British intelligence between the wars was nothing if not disjointed, a jungle of jealous services. Much the largest collector of information about foreign countries was the Foreign Office. The British diplomatic service had become one of the best organized and most professional in the world, notwithstanding the fact that until the present century it was staffed mainly by amateurs, intelligent and not so intelligent. The purpose of the service was to be in permanent contact with other countries, partly to deal with them and partly to know about them. The job was on the whole well done. But the same cannot be said about the intelligence services of the three service departments, which had the narrower task of learning about the size, equipment, organization and doctrines of foreign armed forces. British military intelligence came into being shortly after the Franco-Prussian war of 1870-71 when astonishment over the defeat of France led to the conclusion that a bit more information about the Prussian army might be a good thing. A naval intelligence section was formed in the Admiralty a little later. But these

17

were not distinct intelligence services in the sense that their members were specialists in intelligence. They were on the contrary quite the reverse. They were staffed, on a temporary basis, by officers who had chosen careers in which heroism and drill were far more highly esteemed than knowledge, and a posting to an intelligence section in London, or as an attaché in an embassy abroad, was nearly always uncoveted. The results therefore were poor. The Air Ministry, created after the first World War, suffered the same infirmity. To make matters worse, the three departments preferred to hold themselves separate and, when forced into consultation, co-operated in a spirit of rivalry rather than solidarity.

There were other intelligence services too. Both the Treasury and the Bank of England collected information for economic and business purposes. Their products were complementary. The Treasury would provide government economic missions or travelling businessmen with briefs on a country's resources, finances, industrial and commercial performance, and so on. The Bank, which was in those days a private company uninhibited by official scruples, would add information about the skeletons in the cupboards of Finance Ministers and tycoons, explain who was whose mistress, and provide other similarly useful titbits. I have been told that since being nationalized in 1946 the Bank has felt obliged to stop making itself useful in this way.

Finally, there were the intelligence activities which did not fit into any of these slots. They made up what the man in the street, vaguely and awesomely, called the Secret Service. This famous phrase has no official justification and can be found in no table of organization. The correct name for non-departmental intelligence activities was Special Intelligence Services; but the initials SIS lent themselves to the commonly used Secret Intelligence Service — a name which was neither inaccurate nor inappropriate since the SIS did succeed in keeping its affairs secret. It was distinct from all the other intelligence agencies and had its own funds — an extra piece in the intelligence jigsaw. Its history has never been written, there is no statutory provision for the opening of its archives even after the passing of a hundred years, and so there is no way of telling whether its achievements have matched its reputation. Among its initiates it was referred to as Broadway because that was the name of the street where its headquarters were situated.

At the head of the SIS was its Chief, a serving naval or army officer, designated simply C or alternatively CSS. During the war it was customary, so I was told, to try to track down C at his club in St James's if the need arose outside office hours. The conversation with the club's porter would go something like this: 'I would like to speak to General Menzies, please.' 'I will see if the Chief is in the club, sir.'

C's principal task was hiring and running what the service called agents and other people called spies. His service was small, dealing with a small amount of intelligence and incapable on its own of handling any major new source. But it was alive to the potentialities of new sources — and to the desirability of getting them under its own wing. This is what it did in the case of cryptographic intelligence, an intriguing new source between the wars but largely an unproven one and, in volume, still manageable. By adroit co-operation with the Foreign Office and the service departments, the SIS yoked cryptographic intelligence with the entirely different business of espionage and in doing so created, more or less inadvertently, the inter-service intelligence agency which was to become the brightest jewel in its discreet crown.

# 2 THE ENIGMA MACHINE AND THE POLES

The original version of the Enigma machine was invented and patented in 1919 in Holland and was developed and marketed in the early twenties by a German who incorporated the Dutch invention with his own and gave the machine its name. It was a commercial machine which anybody could buy. Patents were taken out in various countries including Britain and these were open to inspection by anybody who knew where to look for them and had the curiosity to do so.

Among the machine's purchasers were the German armed services. The German navy had been thinking of finding and adapting a machine for its cyphers as early as 1918, and in 1926 it began to use an improved version of Enigma. The army followed suit three years later; there was as yet no air force, but eventually the Luftwaffe used Enigma too and so did the German security services (the police and SS) and other services like the railways. Over the years the Germans progressively altered and complicated the machine and kept everything about it more and more secret. It was to be far and away their most important tool for communications during the second World War, although it would have been superseded if the war had gone on much longer than it did.

Essentially Enigma was a transposition machine. That is to say, it turned every letter in a message into some other letter. The message stayed the same length but instead of being in German it became gobbledegook: it was garbled. That the Enigma machine did this was obvious. The problem was to find out how it performed its tricks. Only if its hidden workings were known, could a decypherer or cryptographer even begin to turn the gobbledegook back into German.

Even when he had got as far as to understand how Enigma worked the cryptographer was still no more than half way to decyphering any particular message. This was because the machine had a number of manually adjustable parts and the cryptographer needed to know not only how the machine was constructed and how it worked but also how these various movable parts were set by the operator at the moment when he

23

began transmitting each particular message. These parts were adjusted every so often — in peace time once a month, later once every 24 hours, and from September 1942 some of them every 8 hours. In addition some parts moved automatically minute by minute when the machine was in use. And, the final complication, each separate message contained its own, individual key and this key was randomly selected.

I shall begin by describing an Enigma machine as it was by the time war broke out in 1939. I shall then describe the motions which a German operator had to go through when he set his machine at midnight and also when he began transmitting each message.

At first glance the Enigma machine looked like a typewriter but a peculiarly complicated one. It had a keyboard like the standard three-row keyboard of an ordinary typewriter but without numerals, punctuation marks or other extras. On the German Enigma the letters were placed in the same order as an ordinary typewriter, beginning with Q on the left of the top line, but in the models made first by the Poles and then by us the letters were in strict alphabetical order beginning with A where you would expect Q. (This was simply an accident. When, as I shall explain in a moment, the Poles constructed an Enigma machine they did not realize that in the electric wiring attached to each key the A wire and not the Q wire ran first into the keyboard. This detail is unimportant.)

Behind the keyboard the alphabet was repeated in another three rows and in the same order, but this time the letters were not on keys but in small round glass holes which were set in a flat rectangular plate and could light up one at a time. When the operator struck a key one of these letters lit up. But it was never the same letter. By striking P the operator might, for example, cause L to appear; and next time he struck P he would get neither P nor L but something entirely different.

This operator called out the letters as they appeared in lights and a second operator sitting alongside him noted them down. This sequence was then transmitted by wireless in the usual Morse code and was picked up by whoever was supposed to be listening for it. It could also be picked up by an eavesdropper. The Germans experimented with a version of the machine which, by transmitting automatically as the message was encyphered, did away with the need for the second operator, but they never brought this version into use.

The legitimate recipient took the gobbledegook which had been transmitted to him and tapped it out on his machine. Provided he got the drill right the message turned itself back into German. The drill consisted in putting the parts of his machine in the same order as those of the sender's machine. This was no problem since he had a handbook or manual which told him what he had to do each day. In addition, the message which he had just received contained within itself the special key to that message.

The eavesdropper on the other hand had to work all this out for himself. Even assuming he had an Enigma machine in full working order it was no good to him unless he could discover how to arrange its parts — the gadgets which it had in addition to its keyboard. These were the mechanisms which caused L to appear when the operator struck P.

These parts or gadgets consisted of a set of wheels or drums and a set of plugs. Their purpose was not simply to turn P into L but to do so in so complex a manner that it was virtually impossible for an eavesdropper to find out what had gone on inside the machine in each case. And, furthermore, to ensure that if P became L this time it would become something else next time. It is quite easy to construct a machine that will always turn P into L but it is then comparatively easy to find out that L always means P: a simple substitution of this kind is inadequate for specially secret traffic.

The eavesdropper's basic task was to set his machine in exactly the same way as the legitimate recipient of the message had set his, since the eavesdropper would then be able to read the message with no more difficulty than the legitimate recipient. The more complex the machine and its internal workings, the more difficult and more time-consuming was it for the eavesdropper to solve this problem.

The Enigma machine fitted compactly into a wooden box which measured about 7 x 11 x 13 inches.

As the operator sat at his machine he had in front of him, first, the rows of keys, then the spaces for the letters to appear illuminated, and beyond these again and in the far left-hand corner of the machine three slots to take three wheels or drums. Each wheel was about three inches in diameter. The wheels were much more than half embedded in the machine and end-on to the operator. They were covered by a lid and when this lid was closed the operator could see only the tops of them. He could easily lift them out and replace them. This is clearly shown in the illustrations.

Although there were three slots for three wheels, there were by 1939 five wheels. The operator had to use three of his set of five. He had to select the correct three and then place them in a prescribed order. This was crucial because the wheels, although outwardly identical, were different inside.

The German navy introduced a four-wheel machine at the beginning of March 1943. At this point the naval operator had six wheels for four slots but the new wheel had distinct limitations: it had to go to the left of the other three and it did not rotate, so that the number of permutations, though much increased by this innovation, was not nearly as large as it would have been if the four wheels had been as freely interchangeable as the three and if all four had rotated. In July of the same year a seventh wheel and fifth slot were added to the naval kit. The greater flexibility and inventiveness of the navy, which was still in evidence at the end of the war, may be ascribed to the fact that it used far fewer machines than either the army or the Luftwaffe. They could therefore be more easily replaced. Most of them moreover were static either in naval HQs ashore or in fleet units. In this context a ship, even when at sea, provides a static home for its machinery in a way which is impossible for an army division or an air squadron, for which moving means considerably more upheaval.

Finally, there were besides the wheels the plugs (in German *Stecker*). These were in pairs. They looked like the plugs on a telephone switchboard. They were added to the machine in the thirties: by the army in 1930, the navy in 1934 and the Luftwaffe in 1935. At first they were at the back but in later models they were in front. There was one plughole for every letter of the alphabet. Each pair of plugs coupled a pair of letters. Putting them in and taking them out to change the couplings was the work of a moment. The number of pairings varied from 5 to 10. In theory there could be 13 pairings of 26 letters but there never were, and for some mathematical reason which I do not understand the maximum number of permutations is obtained when 10 pairings are used. During the Spanish civil war the Germans in Spain used the old Enigma machine without plugs and so did the Italians and the Spanish rebels. We read some of this non-*Stecker* traffic. We also read Italian non-machine cyphers during the war in Ethiopia.

The Enigma machine ran on an electric battery. When the operator of an ordinary typewriter strikes P on his keyboard he mechanically and immediately produces P on the paper in his machine. When an Enigma operator struck his P the effect, though all but instantaneous, was neither mechanical nor immediate. The operator's touch did not move a key and there was of couse no paper in his machine. What he did by his touch was to release an electric pulse and this pulse went on a tortuous journey round the machine before returning to illumine not P but L. The electric current passed through the plug system; then through each of the three removable wheels from right to left, entering each in turn and leaving each of them by any one of 26 different points of entry and exit; and then — after bouncing off a fixed wheel or reflector to the left of these removable three wheels — back from left to right by a different and equally multifarious route, back through the plug system again by a different route, and so to the light for L. The variety and unpredictability of each of these journeyings every time a key was struck were the inventor's pride and the cryptographer's headache.

Each journey from key to light — such was the complexity of Enigma's entrails — might take any one of an astronomical number of routes. The outcome, as shown in the row of lights, was not so multifarious. P could turn into one only of 25 different letters, i.e. 26 minus one. But that was not the point. The point was not what happened at the end of the journey but how it happened. What the cryptographer needed to know was the route, for without being able to establish and repeat the route he could not discover the journey's end.

Enigma, in the form in service when the war began, multiplied its permutations in various ways. First, there was the wheel-order. When there were just three different wheels to place in three slots the number of possible wheel-orders was six. Call the wheels A, B and C: the possible wheel-orders are ABC, ACB, BAC, BCA, CAB, CBA. But when the Germans added a fourth and a fifth wheel for the three slots, the number of possible three-wheel-orders rose from six to sixty.

But that was only the beginning. Not only were the wheels

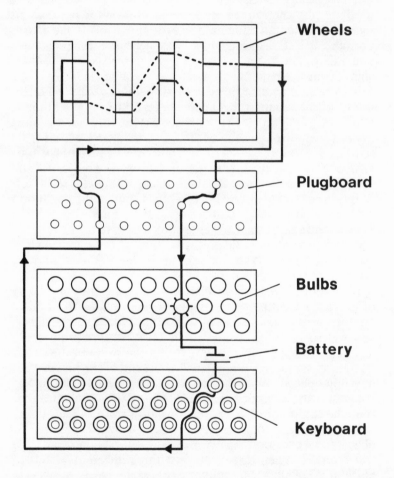

**Wheels**

**Plugboard**

**Bulbs**

**Battery**

**Keyboard**

DIAGRAM OF AN ENIGMA MACHINE

28

not identical; they were not stationary. They rotated. Each had a rotatable rim with 26 different contact points on either side. So each, independently of its fellows, could be set in any one of 26 different positions. And furthermore, every time the operator touched a key the right-hand wheel moved itself on by one notch. When it had done this 26 times the middle wheel began to behave likewise: and ultimately the left-hand wheel too. These shifts vastly raised the number of permutations — the number of different states in which the machine might be at a given moment.

Finally, the extra changes introduced by the plug couplings raised the total to an astronomical figure which, when laid out in full, had 88 digits.

All this sounds horribly complicated and so in one sense it was. But not in another. Although the Enigma machine was a highly complex piece of electrical machinery it was easy to operate, and a brief description of what the operator actually did may help to explain both the machine itself and the cryptographer's task — bearing in mind that the essential difference between the legitimate recipient of an Enigma message and an enemy cryptographer was that, although both possessed and understood the machine, only the former had the handbook which told how the machine's parts were to be arranged each day.

The German operator had to consult his handbook at 0001 hours every day. For every day this handbook gave a succinct set of instructions in four parts.

The first item was the selection of the wheels and the order in which they were to be placed side by side. Each wheel was numbered and the handbook simply gave the numbers of the three wheels to be used: e.g. IV I II. These three numbers also indicated the order of the three selected wheels from left to right.

Next the operator had to fix the rim of each wheel. His instructions were again in figures. They might, for example, read 7 21 12. That meant that the rim of the left-hand wheel had to be fixed at the letter G, the seventh letter of the alphabet; the middle and right-hand rims to U and L. This operation fixed the rims of the wheels in relation to the wheels themselves.

The operator then looked at a third set of three figures.

These told him how to set each wheel on its axis. Over the wheels, once they had been put into the slots, was a pierced lid and when the lid was shut just enough of the wheel emerged to enable the operator to push it round one way or the other. Also, immediately alongside and to the left of where the wheel poked through the lid, was a small spy-hole through which the operator could see one letter on the wheel's rim. The third item in his instructions told him which letter this should be. So, if the handbook read 22 4 15, he rotated the left-hand wheel until V appeared in the spy-hole, the middle wheel until he could see D and the right-hand wheel until he got O.

In 1938 an important change was made at this point. Instead of getting these three letters from his handbook and setting them for a 24-hour period, the operator was instructed to pick three letters himself at random and to make up a fresh three-letter setting for each message. This change was an extension of randomness which, as we shall see in a moment, had always been present in the settings but in a more limited way.

The operator's next and final instruction consisted of pairs of letters: DO LH FM etc. These told him where to put the plugs. With one pair of plugs he coupled D with O, L with H, F with M and so on.

The operator had now complied with the instructions in his manual. His machine was set as it should be for the day. But it still had to be manipulated for each message. The operator had to select at random three letters to constitute the preambular key to be embedded in the message which he was about to encypher and send. He tapped these three letters out twice over, thus getting a six-letter group which he put at the beginning of the message. If, for example, he had thought up LUC, he would tap out LUCLUC, which might be rendered by the machine into PROSHB. He then re-set his three wheels to show LUC, tapped out PROSHB and carried on with the message.

On the eve of the German attack in the west in May 1940, the double encyphering of this preambular key was cancelled. It was, as we shall see, a serious error, for it was the main weapon used first by the Poles and then by the British in their attacks on the daily settings of the Enigma machine.

Such was the Enigma machine. A machine of this kind may in theory be made ever more complex by adding to its parts and this was to some extent what the Germans did when they added extra wheels. But there were practical limits. Most Enigma machines in use during the war belonged to relatively mobile units which had to carry them around in their baggage whenever they moved. An electrical pulse occupies no space but the gadgets in which it functions do — or did in those days. The practical problem therefore was not scientific but technological — making things smaller and lighter. The Germans did have and use more complicated machines than Enigma but they were unsuitable for anybody outside a static office or HQ.

By today's standards Enigma is archaic. Modern technology can produce an infinitely more complex machine which is also infinitely less bulky. Enigma was in its own time a miracle of compact technology but now it has passed into the class of the lumbering gigantosaurus.

*

From 1932 to 1938 German Enigma traffic was read by the Polish secret service. The Poles were almost certainly the only people to do so in these years.

To do this they needed various things. They had to realize, to begin with, that the Germans had started using a machine for their more secret cyphers. Then they needed to discover what sort of a machine it was. Next they had to unravel its workings — a problem in mathematics posed by the machine's engineering. And finally they had to devise ways of breaking each day's settings of the machine.

All these things they did and more. On the eve of war, when the increasing sophistication of the machine defeated their own resources, they passed on all they knew to the French and British, one of the more signal services ever rendered by one ally to another and all the more remarkable in the case of Britain since the alliance was only a few months old.

The Treaty of Versailles of 1919 re-created the Polish state which had been partitioned and finally extinguished by its neighbours at the end of the eighteenth century. The new Poland was in the same vice as the old between Germany and Russia; it was to last only 20 years before being partitioned once more as a consequence of the pact signed by Ribbentrop and Molotov during the night of 23-24 August 1939

31

The new Poland went to war almost as soon as it was born. The Poles attacked the hardly less new Soviet Russian state which counter-attacked and was only prevented from taking Warsaw by French intervention. For their salvation the Poles were also indebted to their cryptographers who were able to intercept and read Russian military wireless traffic from Trotsky downwards. At about this time the Poles were also reading German military and naval cyphers. None of these was a machine cypher but the Poles realized at this early stage how vital to their existence it was to get this kind of intelligence.

When in 1926 the German navy began to use an adapted Enigma machine the Poles were for a time stumped. They divined that the Germans had gone over to some sort of Enigma. In 1929 they bought the commercial model and in the same year a lucky chance enabled them to handle and inspect one of the adapted type which had been despatched from Germany to the German embassy in Warwaw, although they were not able to keep it long enough to dismantle and study its internal workings. Again in the same year they established a special course in cryptography at the University of Poznan and recruited for it a small and select group of young mathematics students. Three of these, working as a team, were then recruited into Polish intelligence — one of them had done a course in advanced mathematics in a German university — and within a year this team broke some Enigma traffic. This was at the very end of 1933.

This success owed something to French help. There has been some controversy about the French contribution to the Enigma story. The principal testimony — which comes from the late General Gustave Bertrand whose book on Enigma was published in 1973 — was at first discounted but has recently been strengthened by General Henri Navarre who worked with Bertrand in the thirties. Bertrand, who was an old man when he wrote his book, seems to have had more than a fair share of personal and chauvinist conceit and he certainly did not like the British; nor did they like him when their paths crossed just before the war. But Bertrand had nothing against Poland, with which France had been allied since 1921, and when in 1931 some useful-looking documents came his way he gave copies to the Poles. They were more useful than probably he knew.

These documents came from a disaffected German whom

the French called Asche and who worked in one of Germany's cypher establishments. Asche was not his real name. Again there is mystery. According to one account he was called Schmidt and had a brother who had reached the rank of general in the German army. According to another and more beguiling story his initials were H E which, being pronounced in French, turned into the German-sounding Asche. In any event what Asche provided in a series of instalments were documents, instructions and drawings relating to Enigma and — eventually — some back settings of the machine over a period of two months. The months in question had gone by but the Poles had intercepted and retained the relevant traffic and so they were able, by applying the settings to the traffic, to solve the workings of the machine. They could now see into it. They would most probably have been able to do so even without this windfall from the French but with it their achievement was accelerated — perhaps by something in the order of two years.

What the Poles were able to do at this point was to reconstruct — first theoretically and then in a factory — the type of Enigma machine then in use by the Germans. They were then half-way, but only half-way, to solving the daily settings of the machine and so reading the traffic.

The problem was to construct an equation embracing the permutations occasioned by the various components which regulated the course of the electric pulse between the keyboard and the lightboard: i.e. the three removable wheels, the reflector wheel and the plugs. This problem was reduced to manageable proportions and then solved by establishing and then exploiting a crucial fact: that the middle wheel did not move until the right-hand wheel had moved 26 times, and that the left-hand wheel rotated even less often. The theoretical attack on Enigma was mounted on the assumption, which was true 21 times out of 26, that the middle wheel stayed put. Given *a fortiori* that the left-hand wheel also stayed put, it was possible to treat all three wheels as a single unit in the conundrum. This made the conundrum manageable.

Knowing precisely how the machine worked and being in possession of an identical version were essential prerequisites to reading the traffic. But they were not enough. In order to take this further step the Poles needed to have an adequate quantity — a 'critical mass' — of traffic and then, by working on this mass of undecyphered traffic, to discover how the German operator had set his machine before transmitting each message.

Here again the French may have given some marginal help. The Polish and French secret services agreed to exchange intercepts. Both were intercepting German cyphered traffic and, since cryptographers can never have enough raw material to work on, this swap agreement was mutually beneficial. It gave the Poles more to play with. There was, however, no exchange of decyphered texts nor is there any evidence that the French decyphered any intercepts. As late as 1939 the Poles were convinced that the French had not discovered how to do this. The Poles, however, began reading German Enigma in 1933.

Their point of entry was the discriminant group. Given an alphabet of 26 letters, the number of three-letter groups available is 17,576. Consequently messages with identical discriminants should be rare. But they were not as rare as mathematically they should have been. It was therefore a fair guess, and a correct one, that obvious sequences such as AAA or ABC were being used over and over again. Further, the rule requiring the three-letter group to be duplicated ensured that each message contained a six-letter group whose first and fourth letters stood for the same original — and likewise the second and fifth letters, and the third and sixth. These pointers served to direct the mathematical skills wherewith the daily settings were broken.

Although the Poles were able from 1933 to read German high-grade cyphers regularly the volume of intelligence which they reaped was not great, since in peace time the armed services used landlines for most of their chat. But they used wireless and cyphers during exercises and also in crises. Thus in June 1934, when Hitler turned on the SA (the brown-shirted Sturmabteilung, in effect a private army) and its leader Ernst Roehm, the Poles intercepted this message: 'To all airfields. Roehm is to be brought here dead or alive.'

In these years the Polish government and general staff learned a certain amount about the German order of battle and mobilization plans, the German armament industry and spies in Poland. They also gleaned a modicum of political information, e.g. which French ministers were expected by the

Germans to collaborate with them. By the winter of 1937-38 the Poles reckoned that they could decypher 75 per cent of what they intercepted. On the other hand they got nothing from this source about the German invasion of Austria in March 1938 because that operation was conducted in wireless silence.

The main problem of the thirties was keeping up with the various changes introduced by the Germans for the purpose of keeping one step ahead of possible decypherers, if only for the fun of it: professional pride fuels progress. The Germans always had great faith in Enigma but they realized that the original commercial version had been freely available and that it was only prudent to go on making their service version more and more complex. The Poles coped with each fresh challenge until in 1938 they lost the German armed services traffic and in 1939 the SS traffic too — which they had continued to read and which they hoped to use as a way back into the more vital cyphers of the German army and Luftwaffe.

What defeated them were two changes introduced by the Germans in September and December 1938. The Poles were not blind to what the Germans had done but they lacked the resources to combat it: they did not have enough money or the time to develop new mechanical counter-measures. The first change, to which I alluded in the last chapter, was procedural. Instead of setting his wheels for the day by following instructions in his manual, the operator was to choose the setting himself at random and to choose a fresh one for each message. The second was the introduction of the fourth and fifth wheels. The Poles correctly divined what had happened. They even worked out the internal connections of each of these new wheels. But the changes overloaded their resources. Although the Polish cryptographers were able to reconstruct these wheels — by a combination of mathematical skills and their existing knowledge of the machine — the mechanical aids which had helped them to solve the daily settings on the old three-wheel type (with its 6 possible wheel-orders) were no longer adequate for scanning the vastly increased number of permutations now embedded in the machine. In practical terms they could not do it. Decyphering required brain power and machine power, and suddenly there was too little of the latter.

35

Faced with the loss of the traffic, and convinced that war was round the corner, the Poles decided to find out whether either the French or the British knew anything that they did not know. They were looking for help. A tripartite meeting was arranged in Paris — whether on Polish or French initiative is disputed. The Polish representatives were instructed to judge for themselves whether the French or British had anything useful to impart. If they thought this was so, they were to put all their own cards on the table and offer full collaboration. If not, not. They formed the opinion that neither French nor British had anything to teach them and so they went back to Warsaw to carry on single-handed.

It has been generally assumed that the Poles were right but it is not impossible that the British went to Paris with the same instructions as the Poles and came to the same negative conclusions about their opposite numbers. I have picked up one or two hints to the effect that the British were not quite so ignorant as they seemed: they had read a primitive form of Enigma during the Spanish civil war. But with only one cryptographer working on Enigma in London it is almost certain that they had got no further and were always a step or two behind the developments progressively introduced by the Germans.

However that may be, the Poles soon decided to take a larger and more generous initiative. In July 1939, with the situation getting grimmer and grimmer, they convoked a second tripartite meeting which was held in a secret hide-out near Warsaw. As in Paris the British were represented by Commander Alistair Deniston, head of what was soon to become Bletchley Park, and Dillwyn Knox, chief cryptographer (and brother of an editor of *Punch* and of an eminent Oxford Monsignore). They were accompanied by a third man who is believed to have been the deputy chief of the Special Intelligence Service, Colonel Stewart Menzies, shortly to become its Chief. He was introduced as Professor Sandwich, a mathematician from Oxford, although his evident unfamiliarity with that subject gravely impaired the disguise.

At this meeting the Poles told all. They described what they had achieved and how. They demonstrated the mechanical aids which they had invented to help their decyphering. One of these, which they called a 'bomba', was a combination of Enigmas yoked together to simulate the workings of the

German machine; but it was not an electronic computer. The other was a glass table, lit from below, on which were piled layers of lettered charts. The light, by shining through gaps in these charts, helped to identify the discriminants of the particular messages. Both machines became inadequate when the Germans provided the extra wheels for the three-wheel Enigma. As parting gifts the Poles presented the French and British with an Enigma machine apiece, the secret German version but manufactured in Poland. The Poles thus handed on a torch — just in time. A few weeks later Poland was wiped off the political map by the German army and air force and partitioned by Hitler and Stalin.

There is a sequel to this story. After the Polish defeat the French asked a number of Poles who had escaped to Rumania to go and work with them at their equivalent of BP which was in a country house at Vignolles 25 miles from Paris. A Polish proposal to invite British cryptographers too was rejected by the French and for the next eight months, until the French too were scattered by the Germans, work on Enigma went on separately at BP and Vignolles. There was some collaboration. Each outfit agreed to give the other any Enigma daily settings which might be unravelled. Vignolles was forced to shut up shop on 23 June 1940. By then the Franco-Polish team had broken 110 Enigma settings, often with considerable delay: a key for 26 October, for example, was broken on 17 January. In all Vignolles read 8,440 German messages. Rather more than 1,000 of these related to the Norwegian campaign, some 5,000 to the campaigns in France. During these months 83 per cent of all Enigma breaks were made at BP. The first was made at Vignolles in January 1940 on the basis of work done at BP.

After the defeat of France in June 1940 the undaunted Poles set up a new centre in Provence in the unoccupied zone of France but when this zone too was occupied by the Germans in October 1942 they fled towards the Pyrenees and Spain. Five of them were captured and held by the Gestapo in horrible conditions. They possessed the most vital secret of the war — and kept it. This was an heroic final service to the allied cause.

# 3 THREE STAGES TO DAYLIGHT

At the basis of the whole Ultra achievement was interception. This was the first stage. Without interception, nothing. And at the basis of interception lay two considerable problems. The first was the physical problem of hearing what the Germans were transmitting. The second was the intelligence problem of sorting out the more from the less valuable traffic in order not to spend time and effort intercepting material which, if and when subsequently decyphered, would turn out to be comparatively uninteresting.

Simply hearing German transmissions was far from easy, even when natural atmospheric hazards were minimal. Audibility improved as the Germans moved to higher frequencies but they transmitted their signals at volumes which were adequate for their own purposes but no more; we were further away. Moreover, these transmissions were to some extent directional: frequently we were awkwardly out of the line of transmission. Hundreds of men and women spent the war glued to earphones at intercept stations, straining to catch what they were not meant to hear. The normal stint was six hours, spent twiddling knobs and hectically taking down in pencil whatever they could.

All this listening was done by the Y services of the navy, army and air force. They listened to radio telephony (R/T) which was the human voice and to wireless telegraphy (W/T) in morse. R/T was used mainly by one-man-bands where the speaker had no other operator alongside him. The principal user was the single-engined fighter pilot conversing with his ground controller or his fellow pilots of the same squadron. E-boats in the Channel used it too. R/T traffic was on VH frequencies and could be intercepted only at much shorter range than W/T. I do not think that we heard any R/T until the German victories in France brought their aircraft and small naval units close to our shores, but R/T interception then became very important both in the Battle of Britain and in the subsequent development of German night fighter techniques. Intercept stations were hurriedly improvised round the east

41

and south coasts, reporting minute by minute to local defence and fighter headquarters and to a central listening HQ at Kingsdown in Kent.

W/T traffic might be *en clair* or in a variety of codes and cyphers, including Enigma. It was mostly on medium or high frequencies. Like so many things the intercept stations were pathetically few when war began; I recollect only four W/T intercept stations in England but this may well be an under-estimate and the service was fairly rapidly expanded as it proved its worth. It was useful to have an empire and so bases overseas where listening posts might be established closer to the enemy's transmissions and at a different angle to them. In the Middle East we had posts at Baghdad, Sarafand, Helio-polis, Alexandria and Aden and these — together with Malta and Gibraltar — were particularly useful for listening to Italian and German traffic in the Balkans and North Africa. When, after the German conquest of Denmark, we in return occupied Iceland we established there Y stations which played an important part in the Battle of the Atlantic. We had also in Egypt a mini-BP which, besides intercepting and locating enemy transmissions and monitoring the rise and fall of their activity (a sensitive herald of coming events), read low-grade cyphers and on occasions Enigma traffic.

The main business of the Y service was plucking messages out of the air but it had also a number of complementary tasks. It located enemy transmissions by D/F (direction-finding) — by taking bearings on the transmitter from two or more inter-cept stations — and so reported not only where they were but when and where they moved. A location might be correct to within a dozen miles. More often it was correct to within 30-50 miles.

The Y operators were also able to recognize individual German operators either — in the case of R/T — by their accents, intonations or other vocal peculiarities, or — in the case of W/T — by their idiosyncrasies in tapping out the morse. A U-boat, for example, could be tracked by identifying her radio operator and taking D/F bearings of his successive transmissions, even when none of his traffic was decyphered. This was invaluable in 1942 when, for ten months, we read no Atlantic U-boat Enigma but were still able to follow the courses of individual U-boats by monitoring their transmissions and identifying the operator. We were in effect tracking the operator.

The air was full of noises and there was nothing to tell which W/T transmissions were German in origin, still less which among the German were Enigma. The only distinguishing features were their frequencies and the call signs of sender and receiver. (There was, however, one way of distinguishing machine-encyphered traffic provided the messages were long enough. In any language some letters occur more frequently than others. There is a pattern. But this pattern does not hold for the arbitrary preambular parts of the messages encyphered by machines, because these parts do not consist of real words. It is therefore sometimes possible to spot the fact that a given frequency is carrying traffic encyphered by a machine.)

Every listener at every intercept station had to be told what frequency or frequencies to cover during his shift on duty. In the early stages of the war this was a chicken-and-egg situation. Nobody had much idea what frequencies would yield the best results and so the interceptors simply intercepted what there was most of. A frequency carrying little traffic had a low priority because the probability was that the paucity of the traffic would prevent the cryptographers from decyphering it anyway. On the other hand the cryptographers had a good chance — or at least a better chance — of decyphering a run of messages when these were long or numerous. And once decyphered their value would be revealed and assessed.

Fortunately most messages had two characteristics besides their frequency. As well as a geographical point of origin which could be located by D/F, they carried the call sign of the sender, who thus identified himself at the start of his message just as a letter-writer identifies himself by the signature at the end of his letter; and the call sign of the recipient, who in this way was told that the message was for him. These call signs were not invariably present but they very frequently were.

By a combination of D/F and call signs, it was possible to establish that a unit using such-and-such a frequency was located at or near X. It was also possible to establish that it was in contact with other units whose locations and call signs could be similarly known. One result was a picture of a network or, in German, a *Stern* (star) comprising a given number of units and covering a given geographical area. Such a star might have the appearance typical of, say, an infantry division. The most active unit would be the HQ,

In every German unit the signals section had a book giving its own call sign for the day and those of all other units with which it might need to correspond. One of the prime tasks of signals intelligence was to reconstruct this book, for if a unit's call sign were known it could be located even if its messages were never decyphered.

Reconstruction was of course unnecessary if a copy of the book could be captured, although the benefits of capture were likely to be transient since German security was usually quick to discover any loss, whereupon the call signs would all be changed. Ironically a capture could be a disadvantage. If intelligence reconstructed a book which was then captured, the Germans would cancel the book and so render nugatory the labours of those who had reconstructed it.

At one point in the war we acquired two copies of the Luftwaffe book known at BP as the Bird Book. One was captured in North Africa where the war of movement yielded this precious piece of loot. The other came from Moscow. The War Office had sent an officer, Major Edward Crankshaw, to try — among other tasks — to do a deal with the Russians on the basis that if they would hand over any useful-looking captured documents we in return would give them the benefit of the output of our splendidly resourceful and brainy intelligence services. Major Crankshaw begged, nagged, bullied and even staged a diplomatic loss of temper, and in response to one or other of these techniques the Russians gave him a great many fascinating and valuable documents. They included a copy of the Bird Book. Crankshaw was laboriously encyphering and signalling to London the extensive contents of this priceless treasure when he received a signal telling him not to bother because London had just received another copy from Africa. As a matter of fact intelligence had at this point substantially reconstructed the book.

When war began the only links between our intercept stations and BP were despatch riders on motor-bicycles. Teleprinter lines were soon installed but to the end of the war most intercepts were delivered by despatch riders who had no idea what they were carrying through fair weather or foul to a modest country house in the middle of England. They too were part of the great army of men and women who made a contribution to Ultra. It was reckoned at one point that the total number of these contributors was around 10,000. Many of them had no inkling of the purport of their often routine and boring jobs.

While interception was an essential prerequisite of decypherment and so of Ultra intelligence, signals intelligence could also be extremely valuable on its own. The preliminaries to Hitler's attack on the USSR in June 1941 provide a clear example. One day two separate messages, D/F'd as coming from the neighbourhood of Warsaw and Cracow respectively, bore the call signs of two construction companies known to be in Holland, where their signals stations appeared to be still active. Intelligence expostulated: something must have gone wrong with the D/F. But the operators stuck to their story: the signals had been put on the air in Poland, not Holland. The next day five more such companies turned up in Poland, shortly followed by administrative elements of the Luftwaffe's Fliegerkorps VIII which was supposed to be in Greece and appeared from the wireless pattern to be still active there. It became obvious that the continuing transmissions from Holland and Greece were spoof. These units had moved, taking precautions to conceal their moves by issuing fake traffic from their old locations. In their new stations they were keeping wireless silence to the extent of not transmitting any messages, but they had to come on the air very briefly twice a day to confirm contact with the centre of the network. This they did by transmitting their call signs and that was enough for them to be spotted and identified. This was not the only evidence of Hitler's intention to invade the USSR but it was compelling and did show that invasion was imminent.

Here is a second example, this time from the end of the war, of how signals intelligence may — independently of any decyphering — bring an element of intelligibility into the babble of the ether and transform it into a picture of the realities on the ground.

It has frequently been said that Hitler's offensive in the Ardennes in December 1944 took allied intelligence by surprise. This is not true. It has also been said that commanders and intelligence officers had become so used to getting detailed information from Ultra about the German order of battle that when Ultra failed to list the formations opposing them they assumed that there were none. While it may well be true that over-dependence on this one exceptional source had its pitfalls, that is an insufficient explanation of the case of the Ardennes.

The battle of the Ardennes was launched on 16 December 1944. Four days later it had failed. The idea for the operation, called by the Germans *Herbstnebel* (autumn mist — the Germans were surprisingly bad at choosing deceptive cover names) was Hitler's and it bore the hallmarks of his military thinking. It was an attempt to seize the initiative from his enemies even at this late hour and was vastly overblown in terms of the resources available to him to carry it out. All the generals involved on the German side regarded the plan as hopeless and did their little best to scale down what they could not stop.

Hitler's idea was to punch a hole in the weakest sector of the allied front, advance at a stride to the Meuse and thence to Brussels, Antwerp and the Channel coast. The key target was Antwerp which had been captured by the 11th Armoured Division on 4 September but was not brought into use as a supply base until the end of November because the Germans kept a hold on surrounding areas. All this is made clear in General Strawson's admirable book *The Battle for the Ardennes*.

Although this last German offensive in the west was foredoomed to failure and in fact aborted in a matter of days, it caused great perturbation on the allied side. The Germans were not thought to be capable of anything of the sort. Allied intelligence had indeed pronounced them incapable. The allies were preoccupied with their own debate on how best to finish off the war and they did not include in their thinking any planned disruption by the enemy. They were worrying about the slackening of their own advance but not about any possible German advance. By the end of November the Americans had taken Aachen, Metz and Strasbourg but the lower Rhine and the Ruhr were still some way off. With their eyes on the Rhine, they gave no thought to the possibility that Hitler might have his on the Meuse.

The German attack was entrusted to Field Marshal Walter Model as Commander-in-Chief of Army Group B, which was one of three Army Groups under the overall command of Field Marshal Gerd von Rundstedt as Commander-in-Chief West.

Model had under his command three armies: 6 SS Panzer Army, 5 Panzer Army and 7 Army, commanded respectively by Generals Sepp Dietrich, Hasso von Manteuffel and Erich Brandenberger. These armies comprised 25 divisions. The preliminary movements of men, equipment and supplies were necessarily considerable. So were the complementary moves by the Luftwaffe: Goering promised 3,000 air fighter sorties a day (although Hitler knew by now that this meant 1,000 at best). The plan was not cooked up on the spur of the moment. An attack through the Ardennes to recapture Antwerp had been foreshadowed by Hitler in mid-September and although Hitler intended to be in charge of it himself, more and more people had to be told about it. At the end of October Hitler, with exceptional solemnity and threats, briefed Rundstedt's and Model's Chiefs of Staff who in turn briefed their superiors. Discussion broadened. Orders were issued. Units moved. Nearly everybody doubted the sense of the plan but nobody doubted that it would be put into operation. D-day was postponed three or four times and each time the circle of those in the know expanded.

One day some time before the offensive, one of my colleagues on the signals side came to me and told me that his section had identified two new wireless networks to the east of the Ardennes. From their configuration these networks looked as though they belonged to full-blown armies. Their corps and divisions could be counted with a fair degree of certitude and located by D/F. They had plainly been told to keep wireless silence which was in itself a significant piece of intelligence. But in those days there was no such thing as total wireless silence because frequencies tended to wander and the HQs of the networks needed to make sure, every twelve hours or so, that their outstations were all present and correct and in full working order. So although these stations transmitted no messages — and there was therefore nothing to decypher — they did pipe up very briefly and provide something to intercept. By observing these contacts our signals people could give a picture of a large ground force in a definable area and apparently holding its breath before embarking on something special.

This example shows incidentally how historians evaluating Ultra from the surviving decodes will miss some of the evidence. Undecoded messages told a story too. This is particularly the case with the German army. For the Luftwaffe our decodes provided full and regular cover of the movements of squadrons. Breaks of German army Enigma, however, were less complete but that did not necessarily mean that we remained in the dark. Signals intelligence could still fill gaps.

In the matter of the Ardennes signals intelligence was not alone in giving warnings of the offensive. We knew from deciphered Enigma that the Germans had ordered special measures to prevent reconnaissance by us over the Eiffel (the hilly country which rises from the left bank of the Mosel). So presumably something was being carefully prepared and hidden there. We knew too from Ultra of transfers of Luftwaffe units from the Russian front to the west and of similar transfers from the northern to the central sector of the western front. We had a great deal of relevant Ultra about the German army's order of battle, while breaks of railway Enigma enabled BP to report the number and size of trains routed to the crucial area. We saw Luftwaffe units suddenly being brought up to strength. We could not give a precise date or the point of attack but we did show that a substantial and offensive operation was in the wind.

When the scare was over and the battle won, the late F L Lucas and I were instructed to write a post-mortem on the part played or muffed by intelligence. We did so, but whether this report still exists I do not know. It is not in the Public Record Office, from which (see Appendix 1) a very high proportion of the most interesting Ultra material is excluded.

A history of signals intelligence would contain many more examples of what could be gleaned even in the absence of deciphering. It would show too how much intelligence could be got simply from monitoring the varying volume of traffic originated by a given headquarters. If the amount went up, either suddenly or gradually over a week or so, that was a fact worth knowing. If a network sprouted additional stations, that too was worth knowing since it implied that additional units had been placed under the command of the HQ operating the network.

But the most fruitful function of eavesdropping was to provide material for decipherers. That is why the despatch riders carried their sheaves of messages to BP where the partnership of cryptography and intelligence laboured to exploit the intercepted gobbledegook by turning it back into German and thence into a weapon against the enemy.[1]

\*

Enigma cyphers were in theory unbreakable except in the sense that every transposition cypher is vulnerable given the time to go through all its possible permutations. For all practical purposes there was no time to do this with Enigma. Each separate message might by itself require an immensity of time.

There was, however, a proviso. To the logical pessimists who pointed out the futility of wasting time on Enigma others retorted that Enigma was unbreakable only if the Germans always kept to the rules — which, being human, they would not. To the blank despair of an older generation of cryptographers younger men, more at home in a machine age, defined their task as getting into a position to spot and exploit mistakes by the other side which were bound to occur.

To do this they had to know the machine that they were up against. This was an essential prerequisite. The Polish gifts to the British cryptographers enabled the latter to skip a stage or two, to move on to another level of the problem. Furthermore, knowing the machine meant knowing not only its nature but also it weaknesses.

For all its merits the Enigma machine had weaknesses which became known to cryptographers when they were able to reconstruct it — the fact, for example, that no letter of the alphabet could ever be encyphered as itself. Z might turn into any letter from A to Y but never did it become Z. The knowledge of a limitation of this kind was useful but by itself it was not enough. Ultimately the ways into Enigma traffic were two: faulty operating procedures and failures to observe the rules.

In the whole course of the war Enigma cyphers were broken in only three ways. The first was the decyphering of the preambular discriminants. The second was the spotting of 'cribs'. Many ingenious cryptographic devices were devised but all of them served one or other of these two main lines of attack. The third way was by spotting re-encodements into an Enigma

[1]Traffic intercepted overseas was sent to BP by wireless after the meaningless German texts had been re-encoded in a British cypher.

cypher from a lower grade cypher which could itself be read.

The attack on the discriminants aimed to disclose the settings of the wheels. A major factor in the success of this exercise was provided by the Germans' own rule that each message's internal three-letter key should be enciphered by duplicating it — that is to say, the rule that LUC should be enciphered (to take the example on page 30) as PROSHB and not simply as PRO. This rule was cancelled just before the invasion of France and the Low Countries in 1940 but not before fatal damage had been done to the security of Enigma.

Both Polish and British cryptographers exploited the fact that, in the six-letter group, the first and fourth letters stood for the same original — and likewise the second and fifth, and the third and sixth. The mathematical problem remained formidably daunting but it was no longer impenetrable and it was penetrated.

The duplication of this internal key was a faulty operating rule. There were also operators who broke the rules. Thus, they were supposed to pick three letters at random and were expressly forbidden to use sequences such as AAA or ABC or words (e.g. the German 'ist') or common abbreviations; but over and over again they ignored these rules. And there was the German operator at Bari who unchangingly used the initials of his girl friend — to whom fortunately he remained faithful. He did a great deal of harm of which he had not the slightest inkling. The more widely Enigma was used, the greater the number of careless operators and the greater the proliferation of human error.

BP cryptographers realized that the Germans would tumble to the inadvisability of duplicating the discriminants and so as soon as they had made their first breaks they began to search for alternative ways into the traffic. The one contributed to the other, for the reading of messages deciphered by the earlier line of attack showed not only that the second and alternative line should be via cribs but also revealed where these cribs were most likely to be found.

A crib was anything that suggested that the message to be deciphered contained a certain phrase. The simplest cribs were of two kinds: a stereotyped message or an address. Weather reports, for example, tended to be couched day after day in similar, even identical, terms; a few obvious words turned up all the time. Further, since they tended to be transmitted at the same time every day, often early in the morning, and came from the same spot, they were comparatively easy to identify. It was again comparatively easy to concoct a series of phrases, one of which would probably turn out to be buried somewhere in the message. We had for many months an even simpler crib — an operator who morning after morning reported that he had nothing to report.

Addresses were another fruitful crib. For example, in North Africa Rommel's HQ would send to Rome every evening a situation report which was despatched from a point whose location was known, on a frequency which was usually known and at an hour which varied little. This report was doubly valuable. What it had to say about the day's operations and about Rommel's appreciation of the position was naturally of the greatest interest, but over and above this intrinsic value Rommel's daily situation report was also the instrument with which BP broke the cypher used by Rommel's Panzer Army and so read not just that one message but all the day's traffic on that network. Somewhere at the beginning this situation report invariably contained the words *An Ida Bison*. Ida Bison or IB, meant Chief Operations Officer.

When the cryptographers thought they had a crib — that is to say, a message containing either a known phrase (*An Ida Bison*) or one which could be approximately guessed (the weather report) — they prepared what were called menus. A menu consisted of the phrase or phrases which they believed to lurk in the message. The next task was to find the precise position of the tell-tale phrase, to slot this sequence into the precise spot where it occurred. A number of possibilities could be eliminated at once. First, the encyphered German text and the menus were placed one below the other. If at any point a letter in the one coincided with the same letter in the other — if a G in the one came immediately above a G in the other — then that position must be wrong since the Enigma machine was incapable of turning G into G. The remaining positions were all possibles. Going through them one by one would be infinitely laborious and time-consuming but at this point a machine took over.

This was the so-called 'bombe'. It constituted the second prong of the attack on the day's settings for that cypher. It

51

worked on the same principle as the 'bomba' constructed by the Poles and displayed by them to the French and British at the meeting near Warsaw on the eve of war. The British bombe was so far altered and refined as to be virtually a different apparatus but nevertheless it was indebted to its Polish precursor. It took the menus and the encyphered text and very rapidly permuted the ones against the other. If and when the one came to correspond with the other, the bombe signalled the solution. This might take anything from ten minutes to ten hours or more — or, if the menus were inappropriate, the bombe would go on for ever without producing an answer.

The bombes were not at BP. Concentrated there they could all have been destroyed at one blow. So they were scattered about the surrounding countryside, tended by Wrens — girls who had maybe joined the navy to see the sea, and seamen, but saw nothing of the former and few of the latter.

The examples of cribs which I have given are very simple ones. They are chosen to explain the processes of breaking machine cyphers in this way. They were like gifts from the gods — and as rare. On most days most cyphers needed far more ingenuity. The cryptographer knew or could guess which German units were talking to each other on the frequencies which carried the traffic using a certain cypher. From his store of knowledge of the decyphered traffic of previous weeks and months he had a fair idea of some of the things they were talking about — order of battle, battle reports, supply, administrative schedules, etc. He might then feel able to make up phrases of the kind that German operations officers or quartermasters habitually used. More fruitful still were the beginnings and endings of messages which in the nature of things were more stereotyped. In practical terms the question arose of how many cryptographers to assign to a particular cypher and how long to leave them at it. There were always other cyphers to be tackled.

At the beginning of the war the number of Enigma cyphers in daily use was, at a guess, not much more than half of dozen. Before the war ended this number had grown to several dozen, all of which changed every 24 hours and in some minor respects every 8 hours. I have heard it said that at one point the German navy alone was using forty different settings of the Enigma machine at a time. On the eve of 'Overlord' the Commander-in-Chief West (Field Marshal von Rundstedt) listed 12 different cyphers to be used in different parts of his command when the invasion came. At about the same time Army Group North — one of the three superior army commands on the Russian front — was using 11.

BP used a number of machines besides the bombe. One of them — which was the joint brain-child of BP mathematicians and Post Office engineers and was brought into use at the very end of 1943 — was the first special-purpose, programme-controlled electronic digital computer ever designed and made. It is, however, improbable that these machines were designed primarily to cope with Enigma. However useful they may have been to Enigma decypherers, they had a greater capacity than was required for the puzzles posed by Enigma and it is a fair guess that their creators had yet more complex cryptographic problems in their sights.

Before the war began the Germans were already using a machine called the *Geheimschreiber* (i.e. secret writing machine). It was used at the highest levels only. Fundamentally it belonged to the same family of machines as Enigma but it was both more complex and more refined. It had at least ten wheels and it transmitted the encyphered texts automatically. It was comparatively cumbersome and this drawback, together with problems of manufacture on a large scale, stood in the way of its widespread use in the field. Nevertheless, in the closing phase of the war BP was becoming fearful that Enigma was about to be extensively replaced by something else, possibly the *Geheimschreiber*. A good deal was known at BP about this machine but whether any of its traffic was ever broken I cannot say — because I do not know.

\*

I come to the third phase of the Ultra story. After interception, decypherment; after decypherment, intelligence. Intelligence takes over when the Enigma messages are back in German.

I have already explained why Ultra intelligence was handled at BP in two different sections, Naval Section and Hut 3. In describing the intelligence work of BP I shall concentrate on Hut 3 for the simple reason that that was where I worked; and for the same reason I shall have more to say about air intelligence than army intelligence.

Looking back one of the more astonishing things about Hut 3 is how few we were. I do not think that it ever exceeded 150 persons, and the total may well have been nearer 100. In its earliest days its chief was a regular serving officer. After him came government by a triumvirate which was not as disastrous as such a recipe might suggest. Unified control was restored in 1942 or 1943 in the shape of an officer from Air Ministry Intelligence who did not at first sight seem the right man for the job but very emphatically was. He is a man whom I would be glad to name, did I not feel that he would find this distasteful. He was unlike other senior people in the Hut, neither don nor schoolmaster, neither professional man nor intellectual. He came from the north Midlands where he was believed to have had something to do with biscuits. He respected and probably admired the mental qualities of his subordinates but was not intimidated by them and showed that since, whether they approved or not, he had been appointed to govern them, he would do so. His internal memoranda were sometimes open to parody but he was a man of firm good sense, he delegated responsibility with generous assurance and most people in the Hut quickly saw how lucky they were to have him. Under his authority my colleagues and I knew exactly where we stood and were completely free to get on with our particular roles, unencumbered by side issues.

Next to him came a team of Duty Officers, one on duty at a time round the clock. The Duty Officer was in charge when the head of the Hut was not on the spot. I shall come to him again. His cubbyhole was Hut 3's principal permanent point of contact with the outside world, whether Ministries in London or commanders in the field.

Below the head of the Hut and the Duty Officers were an assortment of functional sections — first and foremost the Watch which I shall describe below; then the two parallel army intelligence and air intelligence sections called 3M and 3A; a small signals intelligence group; another small group working in the manner of back-room boys on the less urgent intelligence problems; and a communications group of girls who were unremittingly feeding decyphered and translated texts to London and were called for obvious reasons the teleprincesses.

Bletchley Park

The stable block at Bletchley Park

An aerial view of the grounds of Bletchley Park showing the disposition of the wartime buildings

Two surviviors of the wartime buildings at Bletchley Park, one of which was probably Hut 3

The Officers of 3A in 1943 or 1944
From left to right (back) Labertouche, Brooke, Faure, Newton-John, Haskins, Bragg, Ware, Squire (front) Calvocoressi, van Norden, Harrow, Myers, Pilley, Manners-Wood, Rose, Cullingham, Millward

Another view of one of the surviving huts at Bletchley Park

An Enigma machine in its box. In this Polish reconstruction of the German machine the keyboard is arranged alphabetically. In the German models the order of the keys was that of an ordinary typewriter

The keyboard, plate and wheels. The plate showed which letter was produced by each touch on the keys

The wheels shown uncovered. The two wheels not in use are stored to the right of the three which are in their operating slots

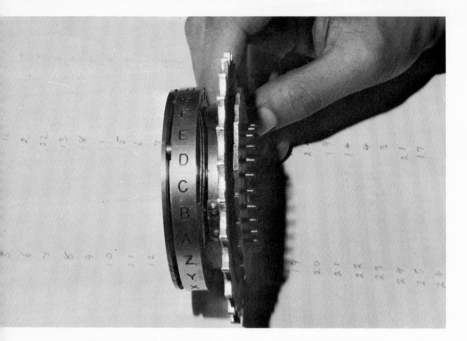

Wheel of an Enigma machine with its rotatable ring

Wheel with its 26 input and 26 output leads

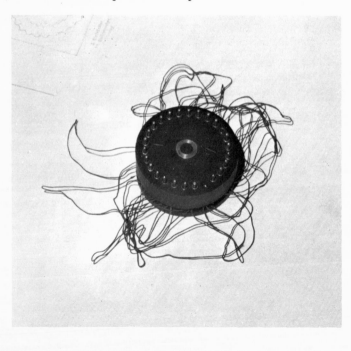

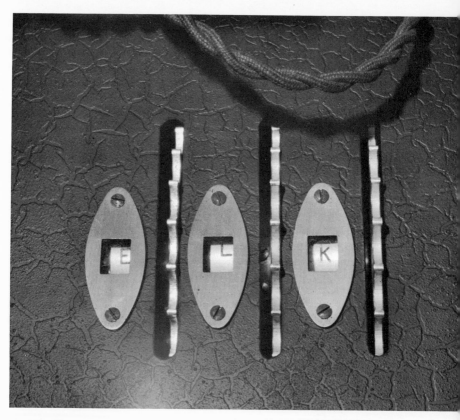

The operator's view of the wheels

The *Stecker* or plugs. These were added in the 30s. At first they were at the back but in later models they were in front

A four-wheel Enigma machine, as used by the German navy after March 1943

Sketch of an early American cyphering machine which was being developed and marketed in the same period as the first commercial Enigma machines

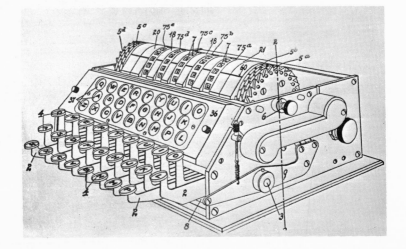

The functions of Hut 3 were to translate the decyphered Enigma material received from Hut 6, to interpet it, and to transmit it to those who needed it. The first of these functions — translation — was performed by the Watch. It sounds simple but often it was not.

What the Watch in Hut 3 received from Hut 6 was a stream of bits of paper. Each German message came on a piece of paper about the size and shape of an ordinary Post Office telegram, or on two or more such bits of paper. The letters were in five-letter groups and ideally they made German words. For example:

Aufkl aerun gsauf gaben fuerd enneu nzehn tenun verae ndert

Which becomes:

Aufklaerungsaufgaben fuer den neunzehnten unveraendert

Or:

Reconnaissance tasks for the nineteenth unchanged.

But a message of this kind could arrive in this form:

Aufkq a--un g-t-f gab-- fmsld enneu nz--- den-d -erxe nd--t

Or worse. (I have made up a simple and typical text, omitting preliminary matter).

A corrupt text might be faulty either because some of the letters were wrongly intercepted in the first place or because they had not been heard at all. In the example I have given it is comparatively easy to restore the text. It is the work of five minutes for an experienced Watch-keeper who is familiar with the traffic on the cypher and network in question. But another message could take five hours, or it could be irrecoverable.

The Watch was in permanent session from the spring of 1940 until the end of the war. About half-way through the war the traffic became so voluminous that a second Watch had to be instituted, normally dealing with back breaks which could no longer have operational significance or with cyphers used by administrative networks whose traffic had background value only — interesting but not urgent. A Watch consisted of about a dozen people sitting round a semi-circular table with the head of the Watch inside the semi-circle and facing his colleagues who were scribbling away or scratching their heads in front of him. They all knew German as well or nearly as well as they knew English. As heads of the Watch schoolmasters were ideal because, besides knowing German, they were pedagogically meticulous and not in the least shy of throwing a dubious piece of work back to its originator as if he were a bad boy and not, as might be the case, a person of considerable distinction in his pre-war vocation. For meticulousness was all.

What the member of the Watch handed to his chief was the Hut 6 text plus his own English rendering of it. On the Hut 6 text he separated the German words by pencil strokes, corrected obviously wrong letters (e.g. q for l in the first group of the example above) and pencilled in his emendations of the missing or faulty groups. He attached his English version which was on a separate piece of paper. The head of the Watch checked all this work as though he had been doing it himself before passing it along to another table in the same room where sat the Military and Air Advisers whom we shall meet again in a moment.

A Watch worked for eight hours and since there were four Watches each of them got a substantial breather every few days. The tempo varied enormously. At times the paper was flowing in from Hut 6 faster than the Watch could cope with it because Hut 6 had broken a number of different cyphers at the same time. My recollection is that by the end of the war Hut 6 was breaking, regularly or irregularly, at least two dozen different Enigma cyphers — army, air, SS and police, railway. The head of the Watch in Hut 3 had to decide what was more urgent and what less so. Today's traffic or yesterday's was normally more important than something a week old but that was not always so. Old intelligence from an active front could be more useful than up-to-the-minute reports from a relative backwater. The head of the Watch sorted the material into different trays, according to urgency, and told his colleagues which tray to dip into first.

There were other times when the flow slowed to a trickle or stopped altogether, but there was generally a backlog to be cleared up and always background reading to catch up with. All Watch members, especially the heads, had to keep themselves fully informed of the material translated by their colleagues and by the other Watches. They were not just translators. They needed to be familiar with the whole intelligence picture in order not to miss a significant clue hidden in the seemingly prosaic message on the scrap of paper before them. They also had to know a great deal of service jargon. The messages were full of semi-technical detail which had to be rendered into its standardized English equivalents. We had on the sidelines one colleague whose job it was to prescribe the correct and precise word or phrase to use for every bit of German equipment from a *Panzerlastkraftwagen* to a nut or bolt. He was a lecturer and lexicographer from Cambridge. His rulings were recorded in a small and well-thumbed card index which stood in a corner of the Watch.

There were other specialists in the wings too, on the lookout for scientific intelligence about German radar or new weapons, cracking cover names given by the Germans to personages or operations, generally monitoring the entire product. This group comprised three or four professors with twice that number of assistants. This tiny extra component was invaluable. At one remove from the hour-to-hour regimen of the Watch and the stressful business of serving commands it was constantly perusing and re-perusing the traffic for inwardnesses which could have been missed; it was free to delve unharassed into conundrums which seemed to lurk in the messages.

Every single text to emerge from the Watch was transmitted to London — to the HQ of the SIS in Broadway and to the intelligence staffs at the three service ministries. The more important messages went by teleprinter but the volume became so great that much of it had to go once or twice a week by courier. This was for the most part background material, less glamorous for the high-ups but invaluable for intelligence staffs.

Hut 3 also communicated directly with operational commands. Signals based on selected Ultra intelligence were sent by Hut 3 to corresponding intelligence officers in the field who knew all about Ultra. These officers briefed the Commander-in-Chief and his Chief of Staff who were however not at first told where Ultra came from. But the tightest security, however desirable for its own sake, has operational drawbacks. The commander who was not let into the Ultra secret could not realize how authentic Ultra was. Consequently he might attach too little weight to it. So the rules were changed and Commanders-in-Chief and their Chiefs of Staff were fully briefed on what Ultra was. This first happened in the Greek campaign in 1941. Much later in the war Captain Alan Pryce-Jones and I did a tour of British and American Commanders-in-Chief on the western fronts in order to tell them what we had in store for them and how we got it. There was some confusion about how to house and feed such lowly officers on missions to Commanders-in-Chief, but these logistical embarrassments apart we spent a fruitful week in the company of the great and admired their intelligent receptivity. Stories about generals' disdain of intelligence are much exaggerated.[1]

The commands served in this way by Hut 3 were HQs at the level of Army and above — and the equivalents on the air side; in other words Ultra did not go to corps commanders or below. At the height of our activity 3M and 3A, who worked extremely closely together, were despatching signals to commands at the rate of one every four or five minutes. As I was part of 3A and eventually head of it I shall confine myself to that section in what follows.

3A consisted of its head, his deputy and their secretary; the Air Advisers; and the Air Index.

The Air Advisers were all RAF or USAF officers. They worked in shifts, in pairs, in the Watch, where they shared a table in a corner with their opposite numbers of 3M. They had, I think, all done a stint on the Watch to begin with. (I certainly

[1]I heard it said during the war that the rules were changed because of Churchill's anger over the loss of Crete, but I no longer believe that this was so. The airborne capture of Crete was an afterthought to the Greek campaign and in some sense an ego trip for General Student and his parachute corps (Fliegerkorps XI). Ultra gave nearly a month's warning of the assembling of the force on the Greek mainland and provided intelligence in detail about strengths, probable landing grounds and even the date of the invasion, all of which was conveyed to General Freyberg. Whether he was fully informed of the nature of the source I cannot say for certain, although I am all but certain that he regarded it as specially reliable. Although it did not enable him to win the battle, it materially helped him to inflict on Student the heavy casualties which deterred Hitler from attempting a similar coup against Malta or anywhere else. Fliegerkorps XI was never again used in the role for which it was put together.

58

did.) Their principal task, which was a highly responsible one, was to send signals to commanders in the field. They saw everything that passed through the Watch. But not everything went to commands — which then would have been swamped. Nor was every piece of intelligence suitable or necessary for all commands. So the Advisers had to exercise discretion in a number of ways. First, they had to decide if a particular piece of information should be signalled to a command at all as well as being teleprinted to London. Secondly, they had to decide which commands should have it; and, thirdly, how fast. Finally it was their business to draft the appropriate signal.

There was one immutable rule. Everything signalled to a particular command had to be repeated to that command's superior HQs. Thus (in army terms) any signal sent to 1 Canadian Army in northern France in 1944 had to be sent to 21 Army Group (Montgomery) to which 1 Canadian Army was subordinated; and by the same token to Montgomery's superior, Eisenhower, at Supreme HQ. All these signals were paraphrases of the originals since it would have been a gross breach of signals discipline and security to transmit the original text, even in translation. Everything stated as fact in the signals was what the Germans themselves were saying, with two exceptions. An Adviser might add a gloss of his own preceded by the word Comment. Thus, to take a simple example, in passing on a Luftwaffe order for an early morning reconnaissance the Adviser might comment that the order was the same as that for the previous day, or several previous days. In doing so the Adviser was both making a point and saving the recipient some trouble in looking up his records. Comments might be quite full: for example, an order to a unit to move to X might carry the reminder that that unit was last heard of at Y or that P and Q were also in the process of moving to X.

The second exception to the rule that signals relayed only the substance of the German texts themselves concerned information which could be derived from the traffic but was not apparent on the face of it. Thus a message which bore no signature might nevertheless be positively attributed to a particular unit by its call sign. In such a case the Adviser was not allowed to say 'Fliegerkorps VIII reports'; nor would it have been sensible to transmit the substance of the message without any indication of where it came from. So a number of conventions were established and in this case the Adviser would draft his signal in such words as these: 'unidentified unit (strong indications Fliegerkorps VIII) reports ...' Similar conventions were used when the text was corrupt. We have seen how the Watch might elucidate a corrupt text but the Adviser was not allowed to treat a restored text, however convincing the restoration, as if it had been uncorrupt. He had to use such phrases as 'strong indications', 'fair indications' or 'slight indications' to convey to his recipient surmises of varying degrees of reliability . All these conventions were perfectly understood at both ends of the line, in Hut 3 and among its clients in the field. They may, however, puzzle a later generation since no explanation of what lies behind these phrases accompanies the documents that have been deposited in the Public Records Office. They were partly a private shorthand but, more importantly, a device for rigorously distinguishing the Germans' own words from everything else. Nobody handling Ultra was allowed to forget the single most crucial point about it: that what it said was what the Germans themselves were saying to and about themselves.

These signals from BP to commands in the field were despatched over a special network which had its HQ about a mile away and used its own specially secure cyphers. I was told during the war that our own cyphers were monitored by our own cryptographers in order to make sure that all the rules of cypher security were being observed. This network was manned by small units called SLUs — Special Liaison Units — under the control of the Secret Service at Broadway in London. Each consisted at first of a single officer with two or three men and they were attached, as inconspicuously as possible, to every command which was in receipt of Ultra. In the last year of war there were about forty of these SLUs with as many different commands. Besides acting as links in the chain of communications the SLUs were also guardians of Ultra's security. It was the duty of the officer, however humble his rank, to insist that commanders and other recipients observe the rules for handling Ultra material. The most important of these rules were that nothing tangible should be taken to an area where there was a risk of capture by the enemy and that the signals themselves be returned to the SLU to be burnt. Breaches of the rules had to be reported back to England. On one occasion a four-star general was reported. The rocket he received by return was quite something.

The traffic handled by SLUs became heavy as the flow of Ultra accelerated and it became necessary not to overburden and clog the links. There were five degrees of priority ranging from Z to ZZZZZ which an Adviser might attach to his signal, always bearing in mind that if he used ZZZZZ too often he would be defeating the purpose of that category. Initially the priority on each signal was determined by the Adviser but he might be enjoined by the Duty Officer to amend his marking. The Duty Officer sat in a little office next to the Watch, from which he was separated by a partition pierced by a glass window. This window would open from time to time to admit his head and some words of advice or question. The Duty Officer was also in touch from this cubbyhole with the Hut's communications systems, both the teleprinters to London and the SLU network to commands in the field. And he was the target for every kind of telephone call, sweet or sour, from chiefs of intelligence, chiefs of staff, the chief of the Secret Service or the Prime Minister. For this job a certain temperament was required as well as a great deal of knowledge.

The second component of 3A, besides the Air Advisers, was the Air Index. This was the central repository of what Ultra knew about the Luftwaffe. Its importance cannot be exaggerated.

It consisted of about two dozen girls and hundreds of thousands of cards. Every individual mentioned in Ultra had a card, every unit, every place. That was straightforward, if laborious and voluminous. Then there were cards for pieces of equipment, cover names, words or phrases which meant nothing at the time but might recur ... the list was endless. As with every index the test of its usefulness was the indexing and cross-indexing of subjects as distinct from names. From first to last the Air Index was designed and nurtured by a strange genius, a man of everyday appearance and attainments who had, and knew he had, a peculiar gift for that very thing: indexing. He was a triangular peg in a triangular hole. He manipulated a proliferating mass of seemingly trivial detail in such a way that its bulk and complex cross-indexing never got in the way of its prime purpose of giving its users what they wanted in the shortest possible time. Each entry on each card had to be

concise and legible: all entries were made by hand in ink. Like
so much intelligence this work could be exceedingly tedious
but it called for constant and thoughtful application.

The head of the shift of indexers received a copy of every
message that passed through the Watch. On it she marked in
red chalk each word and phrase to be indexed and the members
of her shift beavered away at a tempo which might be hectic or
sluggish or anything in between. They never knew what to
expect as they got out of the coaches which, day or night,
brought them into BP from their scattered billets. Most of
them were in their very early twenties. I was at first amazed to
discover how many of them had MAs (at that time a much less
common ornament than now) until I learned that this is the
Scottish for BA. Their labours created a monumental store of
knowledge which was constantly being consulted for quick
answers to straight questions: and for recondite answers to
buried questions. Has Major So-and-So been heard of before
and, if so, what does he do? What sort of a gadget goes by the
name of PX7Q? How many serviceable aircraft were on
Foggio airfield the day before yesterday? Do we know how
much damage was done by Monday's raid on such-and-such a
target? At all hours there was to be found in the Index a handful of people looking for the answers to questions like these.
An Air Adviser would come through from the Watch clutching
a decode which contained a name or a formula which he felt he
had seen before. But in what context? Perhaps it was a year or
more ago and the penny would not drop. The Index would
help.

More than anything else in Hut 3 the Index characterized
what we did there. The cards — about 5 x 9 inches — were
stacked in specially designed stands which stood in rows down
the length of a long room. As the war went on their ranks grew
until they represented a vast corpus of knowledge beyond the
capacity of even the most retentive human memory. So valuable were they that every so often they were photographed and
the copies buried under the Bodleian Library in Oxford for
fear that a bomb should destroy the originals. I cannot discover whether either set still exists.

I believe that it can be said without exaggeration that if from
the middle of the war you had been looking for the half-dozen
persons who knew most about the Luftwaffe in all its opera-

tional and organizational aspects, you would have found them all in England. Hut 3 was certainly the largest contributor to this singular achievement. Yet it occupied only two rooms. The larger, the Air Index, was a long thin room which opened at one end into the Watch and communicated at the other through a hatch with the office shared by the head of 3A with his number two. The Air Advisers, when not on duty in the Watch or off duty altogether, could be found bringing themselves up to date or pursuing some half-solved problem at a spare table in one of these rooms. Across the corridor 3M was similarly housed. The total strength of 3A was, to the best of my recollection, below 50 — of whom of course only a minority was on duty at any one time.

There remains one more ingredient. One day in April 1943 a Colonel Telford Taylor was introduced into Hut 3, the first of our American colleagues. He already knew a good deal about Ultra and it seemed to take him no more than a week to master what we were up to. Others of similar calibre followed. They too were temporarily mobilized civilians and their backgrounds were roughly comparable with our own except that there were rather more lawyers among them than among us. They were slotted into our various sections and in next to no time they were regular members of these sections. When American army and air headquarters were set up in England and later moved to the continent they had their own American Ultra intelligence officers and their own special communications with BP, but at BP itself British and Americans were integrated. In 3A, for example, some of the Air Advisers were American, but all the Advisers served all British and American commands without discrimination. The addition of the American contingent was so smooth that we hardly noticed it. Presumably this was in part due to the sense of common purpose but it must also have owed more than we realized at the time to the personalities and skills of the first Americans to arrive and of the head of Hut 3 and his peers elsewhere in BP.

We members of Hut 3 lived in a series of concentric circles. The tightest of these was Hut 3 itself together with Hut 6 and the Naval Section. This was the circle in which we could talk with complete freedom about what we were doing. The circle bulged slightly outwards to include those in London who were also on the Ultra list. There were, for example, a number of people in Air Ministry Intelligence who would be on the telephone to us several times a day. Most of them were men and women recruited like ourselves into war service in departments which had not existed, or barely existed, before the war. At the level of Wing Commander or Group Captain and above they were regular RAF officers, but below that level they were almost all wartime recruits with whom we were in constant touch and whom we got to know personally quite well. It is impossible to imagine Hut 3 without the scrambler telephone. Its invention meant that we could discuss the latest detail or puzzle with colleagues in the Air Ministry in the same way as we discussed these matters among ourselves in the 3A office.

The second circle was BP itself. Outside the sections I have mentioned a few senior persons knew all about Ultra. The rest did not and they were the great majority of BP's inmates. For Hut 3 most of BP was the outside world. It was an outside world which, by the end of the war, comprised several thousand people, most of whom we knew neither by name nor by sight. All these people were deposited at BP by coaches at fixed hours and left again at fixed hours to be taken back to billets scattered round Bletchley within a radius of about fifteen miles. On arrival they scuttled into their huts and stayed there at work until it was time to board the return coach. The main exception to this dispersal was the lunch break or, for shift workers, visits to the canteen for other meals. The canteen, built under the impact of BP's population explosion, was at the edge of the grounds some two or three hundred yards from the mansion itself to which, after lunch, people might drift for coffee, light recreation or simply in fine weather to sit on the grass between house and pond to relax for half an hour or organize some extra-curricular activity from a picnic to a performance of *Figaro*.

BP was a very unmilitary place. It paid scant attention to the hierarchies either of military rank or of the civil service. Its chiefs were civilians on the payroll of the Foreign Office and there were also the pre-war veterans, mostly cryptographers. But these were vastly outnumbered by the wartime intake which proved to be very much greater in numbers than anybody had ever imagined. If unconsciously, BP took its tone from them. Those of us who were commissioned officers wore uniform only when we felt like it — or when some top brass was expected on a visit. BP was not a place where people went around saluting one another. Rank might be coveted for the extra pay or, in the latter part of the war, as a mark of recognition, but it did not affect personal relations. It never seemed quite real, partly because the war itself never seemed to be anything but an interlude. Looking back I remember no talk about how long the war was likely to last but I do not think that anybody felt that it was going to last long enough seriously to divert the course of our lives. I suppose that until near the end we would have surmised that it would last a few years, but only a few. This was subconsciously important. It meant that there was very little jockeying for position among us. Our futures and our war work were unrelated.

There is a set of papers which, provided it has not been destroyed, could admirably illustrate Hut 3's peculiar amalgam of freedom and rigour. Every eight hours Hut 3 shed a skin. The Duty Officer, the Watch, the Indexers, the Advisers, the teleprinter operators, the internal messengers, all went off duty to make way for the next shift. During that eight hours a sheaf of translated decodes had been teleprinted to London.[1] Each one was on a separate foolscap sheet, known as a T/P. On the same sheet were any comments and elucidations which the Advisers might have appended and also the text of the signal (if any) sent to commands overseas on the basis of the decode with, finally, details of the priority given to the signal and a list of the commands to which it had been sent. One set of these T/Ps was delivered to the 3A office.

Both the head of 3A and his deputy went through the T/Ps with a hypercritical eye and wrote comments on them. These comments might query an interpretation, indicate an omission or possible further line of inquiry, take issue with the Adviser's handling of the message — or praise it — and so on. Every Adviser was required to read every T/P in this marked set and to add, if he so wished, his own riposte to any comment or criticism which had been made. These criticisms could be quite

[1]The daily count of T/Ps varied, so far as I can recollect, between 50 and 100 but I have no way of checking these figures which may be quite wrong. The bulk of the decoded material went to London not by teleprinter but by bag. These had gone through the Watch in the same way as the more important T/Ps but they were mulled over in 3A and by the Advisers at greater leisure.

sharp and it was necessary for the maintenance of standards that they should be, but they did not have the character of a dressing-down or (except rarely) a rebuke: nobody stood, even mentally, to attention. The interchanges constituted a debate between equals which generated remarkably little ill-feeling. It did not occur to an Adviser under fire to remind his colleagues that it is human to falter at the end of a gruelling eight-hour shift. Still less would an Adviser who disagreed with criticism of himself stifle his riposte because his critic held a higher rank.

The third and outermost circle in which we lived were the billets, pubs and villages where we laid our heads and, in theory at least, got away from it all. Some of us acquired houses where, unless they were very small, the billeting officer quickly implanted billetees. In the earliest days, before the weekend fell victim to crueller wartime routines, new recruits to BP would return to their colleges in Oxford or Cambridge; there was one Cambridge college which contributed so many Fellows to BP that they were said to be incautious in their talk at high table, forgetting that there were among them some who knew nothing about BP. In the villages of Buckingham and Bedfordshire strangers appeared, either to be shunned with a half-awed distrust or to be taken up by kind hostesses willing to dispense hospitality in exchange for good talk. But the privations of war — notably petrol rationing — fragmented social activities. One of the consequences of war is to allow the workplace to usurp many of the hours which a more tranquil dispensation allots to domesticity.

# 4 THE USES OF ULTRA

When war began it was by no means obvious that Ultra would be of much use, even if it could be got. In the rest of this book I try to show where and how it became a major war-winning weapon.

The first fruits were meagre, scattered and not very exciting. They came from breaking the cypher used by the German Wehrkreise. These were the static army administrative regions or home commands, each corresponding to an army corps, into which Germany itself was divided. These scraps of information dealt with recruiting, travel arrangements and so on. Each Enigma cypher was given a name at BP. This one was called Green. It was not at all promising.

The first indications of Ultra's further potentialities came during the invasion of Norway which was launched on 9 April 1940. This operation was concerted and conducted by an inter-service command created for the occasion under the overall authority of the Supreme Command of the Armed Forces (OKW). It was given its own cypher which we called Yellow, and we read a certain amount of it — about 1,000 messages in all. It was broken within a week of the beginning of the campaign and we read it regularly for a month, although with some delays. Unlike Green, Yellow provided operational intelligence and the first convincing evidence that Enigma breaks might be operationally valuable, provided cyphers like Yellow could be broken not only regularly but more promptly. It was therefore a portent and it encouraged those who argued that if BP could get this much it might very well get more. But for the fighting in Norway Yellow's operational significance was virtually nil. Neither BP nor the wider world of intelligence was as yet equipped to understand or handle Ultra. Staffs were small and untrained, organization non-existent. Before the invasion such clues as we had to German intentions came from more traditional sources — agents or photo-graphic or visual reconnaissance. Agent's warnings were numerous and prompt and so were warnings from diplomatic sources. The first of the long-range Spitfires fitted with cameras in place of guns had taken pictures of Kiel; the *Scharnhorst* had been seen on the move; photographic cover was, however, thin. But all these clues were largely wasted, and about the timing of the invasion we knew nothing.

On 10 May, precisely a month after going into Norway, Hitler's ground and air forces attacked the Low Countries and France. Between that date and the signing of the French armistice on 22 June Ultra rendered some service although again its practical consequences were minimal. But during these weeks a momentous event took place. On 22 May BP began its uninterrupted penetration of the principal Luftwaffe cypher — Red. This cypher was used by countless Luftwaffe units in every theatre where the Luftwaffe operated. There had been sporadic breaks of Red from the very beginning of the year but on 1 May the Germans had made changes to the Enigma machine which countered these successes. The importance of 22 May lay in BP's prompt surmounting of the new difficulties and in the fact — not realized at the time — that we were never again to lose Red. It became the constant staple of Ultra for the rest of the war. From this point it was broken daily, usually on the day in question and early in the day. Later in the war I remember that we in Hut 3 would get a bit techy if Hut 6 had not broken Red by breakfast time.

Intelligence is one thing and making use of it is another. Forewarned is not always forearmed. Operational intelligence is useless if operational weapons are lacking. During the fighting in France a decyphered message ordered a German air unit to bomb a target designated by a cover name. It so happened that the German commander to whom this order was addressed had forgotten what the cover name stood for. So he had to ask. He was told that it meant Paris. But nobody could make use of this piece of information for lack of guns and aircraft. Moreover, by the time we began to read Red daily the battle for France had been irrecoverably lost. In fact Red's greatest service may well have been its incontrovertible demonstration that this was so, that the Germans could not fail to overwhelm their enemies, and that for Britain to throw more forces into the battle would be to throw them away. (Unknown to us the German victories were facilitated because the Germans were reading French army cyphers which told them how strong — or weak — French and British units were and how they were being manoeuvred in the face of the German advances.)

There was too in these early days another serious deficiency on our side. To be useful intelligence requires interpretation and therefore practised intelligence officers. In 1940 Ultra was scrappy and puzzling. What there was of it was frequently not understood. Nor, by definition, was there any body of earlier intelligence with which to collate and supplement it. There is, for example, the story of the man who walked into a colleague's office with a handful of Ultra decodes, threw them down on the table and asked what on earth was the point of the stuff. The messages consisted entirely of figures. To the untrained eye they might be anything — or nothing, mere practice doodling. On this occasion the man behind the desk had one of those flashes which intelligence officers are paid to have. What if the figures were co-ordinates, map references? Assuming that they might be, a few minutes' work with a map showed that they all pin-pointed airfields. Given what was known about the frequencies and call signs associated with the senders of the messages, quite a lot could be made of such seemingly random and trivial rows of digits. Later in the war there were many more puzzles of this kind but experienced intelligence officers, who had become familiar both with the contents of the traffic of such units and with the way the Germans habitually did things, were able to unravel the riddles. We will find examples when we come to the daily returns made by German army and air units.

Red was a comparatively easy cypher to break because its daily volume was considerable and it carried a number of early morning cribs. But in 1940 what it yielded was still fragmentary. With the lull after the fall of France most Luftwaffe units reverted to landlines. German army Enigma was still unbroken. On the other hand the importance of Enigma had risen. As Hitler overran Europe we lost much of our diplomatic reporting and even more of our agents. We were taking no prisoners of war. Photographic reconnaissance was hampered by the range of available aircraft as well as the normal hazards of weather and enemy interception. These were our darkest hours in more senses than one.

The second half of 1940 brought the threat of invasion, the Battle of Britain and then the bomber blitz. There is contro-

71

versy over the extent of Ultra's contribution to victory in the Battle of Britain. Some extravagant claims have been made. In my judgement they are wrong. Ultra gave valuable help in working out the order of battle of the Luftwaffe, above all the locations of its units and to some degree its overall front line strength. But it did not sufficiently correct current estimates of the Luftwaffe's total strength or its normal standards of serviceability, both of which were greatly exaggerated; nor could it provide information about aircraft production in German factories. Ultra showed that a big air effort was coming against England and gave clues to its scale, but it could not help with dates. Once battle was joined, low-grade cyphers and radio chat (which was also intercepted) became more important tactically, as was frequently the case throughout the war. In the battles in North Africa, to take another example, what a commander wanted to know was what quite small units on the other side were doing and saying, and this information came across in tactical exchanges of a strictly local and ephemeral nature, not the sort of stuff that was encyphered on Enigma.

About 'Sealion', the invasion of England that never took place, Ultra made similar contributions. It did not provide precise details either about the numbers of the barges which were being assembled in Channel ports or about the all-important question of where they were to make landfall on this side of it; nor did it give invasion dates. But once more its growing mastery of the Luftwaffe's order of battle enabled it to assess the scale of the threatened onslaught and to warn that it seemed to be imminent. Ultra also disclosed a singularly material item: the disbanding of the staff which had been specially constituted by Hitler to control the invasion. The disappearance of this staff meant that the invasion was off, at least for that year. This piece of information was a strategic plum.

Although Britain was alone against Hitler in the Battle of Britain, there was another battle going on at the same time. This was the war with the Italians in north and east Africa, begun by Mussolini's declaration of war in June. The need to reinforce these battle fronts was hardly less urgent than the need for victory at home. Wavell was getting help from India, Australia and New Zealand but he desperately needed tanks from Britain too. The question was how many and how soon. A first small contingent of 50 was despatched to him on 22 August but since the passage round the Cape took five to six weeks, decisions about further reinforcements were continuously clamouring to be made. In this extraordinarily difficult dilemma it was a tremendous relief to know for certain, before the end of October, that 'Sealion' had failed and that in his own mind Hitler had acknowledged as much. Although Hitler kept up the pretences Ultra demolished them. Hitler ordered a deceptive spoof in order to maintain the illusion that his special invasion staff was still in business but Ultra, which had long ago spotted the staff and shown what it was for, then revealed its removal.

Churchill's boldness in sending tanks to the Middle East while the British Isles were still under siege may be likened to the action of the Senate of Rome when it despatched an army to Spain while Hannibal was still at the gates of the city. The praise is deserved; a lesser man would have quailed. But it is also true that during that summer Churchill could not have left Wavell without reinforcements and that from October he was acting with a hidden assurance which he owed to Ultra. (The War Office was more circumspect. It too had a special invasion staff, created to co-ordinate intelligence about Hitler's preparations. In spite of Ultra's revelations this staff was kept in being until 1943.)

The cancellation of 'Sealion' was followed by the blitz which lasted through the winter of 1940-41 and up to the redeployment of German forces in preparation for Hitler's attack on the USSR, and it was at this point that Ultra's impact on operations became for the first time cardinal.

The blitz was an attempt to destroy British morale, industry and ports. It had to be made at night and because it had to be made at night the German bombers had to have navigational aids to get them to their targets. By understanding what these aids were and interfering with them British scientific intelligence helped to bedevil the bombers and get them to drop their bombs in the wrong places.

The aids used by the Luftwaffe were three: Knickebein, X-Gerät and Y-Gerät. These were all radio beams, although even this basic fact was not known for certain to begin with. The beams were used to guide a pathfinder force — KGr 100 which used Knickebein and then X-Gerät, and III KG 26 which used Y-Gerät. With Knickebein the pilot flew along a beam, keeping station with the help of gadgets in his aircraft which told him if he were straying to one side of it or the other. At a predetermined point his beam intersected with another. This intersection pin-pointed his position near the target and from there he steered a course by dead reckoning or map reading. X-Gerät was a refinement of Knickebein which incorporated the speed of the aircraft into calculations which governed the exact moment for the release of the bombs. (It was first used in the raid on Coventry on 14 November.) With Y-Gerät the air-crew, although still flying the aircraft, were no longer doing the bombing because the apparatus transmitted its calculations back to base and enabled the bombs to be automatically released.

A month or two before the blitz began BP broke a special Enigma cypher used by KGr 100 for communicating with the technical research unit which developed all these beams. With the aid of this traffic Dr R V Jones, the scientific adviser to the air staff, was able to reconstitute the Knickebein system within about two weeks and so devise counter-measures to jam or distort the beams. Jones was a young physicist who was recruited for scientific intelligence work during 1939 when it occurred to somebody that something ought to be done in this virtually non-existent branch of intelligence. By a coincidence he reported for duty on the day war broke out. Ultra was not his only source of intelligence but Ultra, being what it was, set the seal of fact on his surmises. In his book *Most Secret War* Jones relates how a single Ultra message transformed his work. It was neither a long message nor an explicit one. It simply pin-pointed an object on the Channel coast. There was nothing in the message to show what the object was, but the context made it sound interesting and it was immediately photographed. Without the message it might have gone unnoticed and could not have been located. It turned out to be a Knickebein and the photographs finally removed all doubts about the nature of the aids which Jones was working to iden-tify and counter. On this and other occasions Ultra gave Jones the certainty which he needed when formulating the advice which it was his duty to tender to the air staff and war cabinet. Ultra also pin-pointed the five or six bases which sent out the

Knickebein beams and it produced the first reference to X-Gerät while this system was still at the experimental stage. It provided comprehensive technical details, although not all of them were fully understood at once and the counter-measures to X-Gerät were not wholly successful. The existence and nature of Y-Gerät were also revealed by Ultra during the summer of 1940, and all this background intelligence was supplemented by operational intelligence when the blitz began. Ultra then gave the frequencies to be used by the beams for the coming night's raids and for the exchanges between the pilots and their base which normally came on the air about an hour before take-off.

These achievements helped to abort or misdirect a number of German raids. Neither Ultra nor other sources of intelligence nor the RAF nor the anti-aircraft defences could prevent the Luftwaffe from doing enormous damage to English cities that winter, for the German attack was much stronger than the British defences; but death and destruction were to some extent reduced. The Germans' main obstacle was their difficulty in finding their targets in the dark. Intelligence, in which Ultra played a significant part, succeeded in interfering with the aids which the Germans developed in order to find their way.

The most famous episode in the blitz was the raid on Coventry on 14 November 1940, about which a few words must be added because false stories have recently given this tragedy a second notoriety. It has been alleged that we knew in advance from Ultra that Coventry was to be attacked that night and that in order to avoid compromising the source Churchill refused to allow action to be taken to minimize the death and destruction. None of this is true. Ultra never mentioned Coventry. The question of safeguarding Ultra never arose.

Three days before the raid an Ultra message, addressed in the original to KGr 100, gave a list of frequencies and other procedures for an operation called 'Moonlight Sonata'. It was evident from the message that the operation involved an exceptional effort. No date was given. No target was specified but certain target areas were referred to in code. From other available evidence these were believed to be areas in and near London. In a separate section of the message appeared the

75

single word *Korn*. In retrospect it has been suggested that Korn stood for Coventry — on the grounds that the initial letters were the same, a common German practice with cover names. I myself have never been able to see why, in this solitary context, Korn should have designated Coventry or any target whatever; but it may have. A day or two later a routine KGr 100 message set out bearings from a series of beam emplacements. The bearings intersected at Birmingham, Coventry and Wolverhampton. These targetings indicated that, at some unspecified future date, these three cities were likely to be bombed, if only because they were being added to a target list (which seemed already to contain several dozen names). At almost the same time a prisoner stated that Birmingham and Coventry were shortly to be bombed. His was the only specific reference to Coventry by name.

These pieces of information were taken to portend a major raid at the full moon (15 November) with London as the main target but the industrial Midlands as a possible alternative. Certainty would have to await the activation of the beams which could be relied upon to point to the target a few hours before sunset. Between 3 and 4 p.m. on 14 November monitoring of the beam frequencies showed that Coventry was to be the night's main target. The usual counter-measures were taken, including special measures which had been prescribed some weeks earlier, although one of these measures — the jamming of the beams — was rendered largely ineffective by a mathematical error. In addition 'intruder' operations were flown that night against targets all the way from Berlin to the west coast of Brittany. Churchill, so far from pondering whether to save Coventry or safeguard Ultra, was under the impression that the raid was to be on London.

Later in the scientific war Ultra again played a contributory role in collecting intelligence about the V-weapons. The plans for these weapons were known from the very beginning of the war and so was the place — Peenemünde — where the research and experiments were conducted. It was crucial to discover the range of these weapons, their accuracy, the weight of explosive in each warhead, the number that the Germans would be able to fire off per day, and above all when they would begin. The main sources were photographic reconnaissance, agents and the (non-Enigma) codes used by the companies engaged in tracking the flight of each experimental launching from Peenemünde. In the case of the V2 there was also valuable information from the pieces of a rocket which landed in Sweden and established conclusively and for the first time that this weapon, unlike the V1, was not radio-controlled. To all this Ultra contributed. It was not a self-sufficient source but it was a very valuable one.[1]

*

The events of 1940 — the Battle of Britain, the cancellation of 'Sealion' and the containing of the German night blitz against English cities — decided that the war would go on. Hitler lost his bid to eliminate all that survived of his enemies to the west of him. Nevertheless in 1941 he turned to the east and invaded the USSR in June. Then at the end of that year, after Pearl Harbor and because of it, he declared war on the USA, an act of folly which revitalized the war in the west at a moment when his first campaigns in the east had failed to destroy the Russian armies or take Moscow or Leningrad. (Hitler brought the Americans not only into the war but also to BP. The immensely able American contingent made BP inter-allied as well as inter-service.)

But although these two acts in 1941 sowed the seeds of the destruction of nazi Germany the seeds were a long time germinating. Both in the east and the west, in the USSR and the Atlantic, 1942 was a good year for Hitler. His armies could still hope for victory over the Russians and his U-boats were making the Atlantic increasingly impassable for supplies to Britain and for the transfer of American armies to Europe. In Africa too Rommel had the better of the argument for most of the year. The war was being waged on a periphery far removed from Germany itself.

Then in the winter of 1942-43 this periphery cracked at three points: in North Africa and the Atlantic and at Stalingrad. At

[1]The most extraordinary document in the scientific intelligence war was the so-called Oslo Report which was delivered anonymously to the Secret Service in November 1939 and contained information about German scientific developments over the whole course of the war. The author of this report is still alive. His name is known but I do not know it.

two of these points Ultra made a very big difference indeed. And by then it had both organized itself at BP and impressed itself on the world of operations outside the BP compound.

Ultra came into its own in the first months of 1941 through the richness and promptitude of the information which it gave about the movements of stores, staffs, troops and aircraft into south-eastern Europe, information in which Luftwaffe Ultra was supplemented by regular breaks of transport or railway Enigma. These enabled us to follow practically day by day the German occupation of Rumania and then Bulgaria, pointing unequivocally to the invasion of Greece which, after sundry delays, was launched on 6 April. It was in these months that confidence in Ultra was established, together with increasing expectations of it and reliance upon it.

Throughout the war Luftwaffe cyphers were more frequently and more continuously broken than others and the volume of air traffic into Hut 3 exceeded army traffic. But air cyphers were not confined to information about the Luftwaffe. As we have just seen they provided grist to the mill of scientific intelligence and they betrayed the movements of shipping between Italian and Greek ports and North Africa. They also told us about the German ground forces in Africa and elsewhere. Here are two examples.

One of the greatest benefactors of Hut 6 and Hut 3 was the Flivo — the *Fliegerverbindungsoffizier*. The German ground and air forces had developed co-operation to a high degree. In fact the Luftwaffe, in spite of being a distinct and independent service, was cast first and foremost in the role of army support. Both in the early campaigns in the west and in North Africa the Luftwaffe was used in close support of the kind of mobile ground tactics which the German army, particularly its tank generals, had perfected. Hence the importance of liaison between the two services and of the Luftwaffe's liaison officers at army HQs — the Flivos.

The job of the Flivo was to report to his parent Luftwaffe unit the plans of the army unit to which he was attached and its appreciation of the situation. To do this the Flivos in the Mediterranean theatre used a cypher called by us Scorpion. Now the settings prescribed for Scorpion were, by an incredible stroke of careless indiscipline, the same as the settings which had been used earlier for a different Luftwaffe

78

cypher called Primrose (which was the cypher of the Luftgaue, the static home regions of the Luftwaffe and its equivalent of the army's Wehrkreise). Hut 6 had been reading Primrose and it quickly tumbled to the fact that the current Scorpion settings were old Primrose settings. So for a time Scorpion presented no problems. Most of Scorpion was intercepted in the Middle East and a small party was sent from BP to Egypt to do the decyphering on the spot.

The Flivo continued to figure prominently in BP's affairs throughout the war. Here, for example, is a signal sent by Hut 3 with the highest priority to nine American and British headquarters at 1226 hours on 23 June 1944. The information relayed came from the headquarters of the German 7 Army in northern France and was only 14 hours old:

> Appreciation according Flivo seventh army 2230 hours 22nd. Heavy lorry traffic and increased supply flights in right sector of I SS Panzer Corps indicated possibility of allied intentions to attack right sector of corps as well.

A strange bonus from Luftwaffe traffic occurred soon after Rommel's arrival in Africa in February 1941. Rommel got his forces into action faster than anybody expected. This was the beginning of the nervous admiration which became typical of the British reaction to Rommel, and London was now most anxious to discover whether his further plans were cautious and limited or whether he might make a dash for Cairo, Suez and Asia. But BP was still not reading army Enigma.

Berlin too was worried. Rommel was an unpredictable general who did not always do what he had said he would do. If opportunity beckoned he would change his plans, sometimes without bothering to say so. The Chief of Staff of the Army, General Franz Halder, was distrustful of Rommel and fearful too of the demands he might make if he got the bit between his teeth. So towards the end of April Halder sent his Deputy, General Friedrich Paulus, to find out what Rommel might be up to. Paulus stayed two weeks in Africa and he and Rommel agreed the strategy which was to be pursued. Paulus put the agreement on the air to Berlin. For some reason which I have not been able to fathom he used the Luftwaffe cypher. So we came into possession of an important document which we would never have seen if Paulus, who was after all an army

79

general reporting to the army high command, had used an army cypher.

The strategy adopted was a cautious one. Rommel had made in April a partially successful attack on Tobruk, in which he penetrated — but did not hold — its outer defences. This venture was not to be repeated. So it seemed that Tobruk was probably safe for a while and Cairo all the more so. Paulus's report also exposed the supply problems which were already beginning to plague the Germans in Africa, and Wavell was able to plan his counter-offensive in the knowledge of these difficulties. What Wavell did not know was that the Germans in their turn were reading British low-grade battlefield cyphers, thanks to which (as well as to his own skills) Rommel was able to survive. Churchill's loss of confidence in Wavell was sharpened by the disappointing outcome of these counter-attacks which, to anybody seeing only one side of the intelligence contest, ought to have disposed of Rommel.

German army cyphers were consistently more difficult to read than Luftwaffe cyphers. The first breaks were made in African traffic in the latter part of 1941. They were reinforced at the end of the year when some cypher books giving back settings were captured in the course of Auchinleck's truncated operation 'Crusader' in Cyrenaica in November. By collating the information acquired in this way with the backlog of undecyphered material in its cupboards Hut 6 was able to familiarize itself with this traffic and so break the current correspondence of Panzer Army Africa. But successes were erratic. At one stage the traffic was lost for several months and BP did not master it reliably until the spring of 1942. Even then it was not always decyphered promptly. There were two main cyphers: Chaffinch and Phoenix. The first was used between the army HQ and its corps and the second between corps and divisions. They were never easy to break and I do not believe that Chaffinch was often broken in less than 48 hours. The information which they supplied was supplemented by the breaking of Bullfinch, the parallel cypher to Chaffinch used in Tunisia by von Arnim's 5 Panzer Army from its arrival there at the end of 1942 to the final defeat and surrender of all the German and Italian forces in Africa in May 1943.

By far and away the most valuable intelligence derived from these cyphers was what they told us about the enemy's order of battle and the capabilities of his ground forces, unit by unit. Divisions reported to corps, corps to army, and army back over the sea to the HQ in Rome of Kesselring as Commander-in-Chief of the whole southern theatre, a post created for him in the autumn of 1941. The reports, usually prepared and despatched at the end of the day, were in the form of abbreviated pro formas. They were not self-evident but rather examples of the sort of puzzle which, as I mentioned earlier, requires elucidation by a practised and pertinacious intelligence officer. Between its preamble and signature such a message might go something like this:

1 15 2 7 3 12 4 0 5 33 6 203 7 82[1]

At first sight only one feature of this series leaps to the eye: the first and alternate numbers are the arithmetical sequence beginning with one, and so they almost certainly indicate paragraph numbers. The message may then be re-stated and punctuated to read:

1. 15
2. 7
3. 12
4. 0
5. 33
6. 203
7. 82

If this is correct, the unit reporting has 15 of something, 7 of the next thing, 12 of the next and so on. But what are these things? The unit used the same pro forma evey day and by studying these returns over a period and collating them with other information about the unit in question, intelligence could arrive at the answers. An army unit would need to report its strength of serviceable tanks, armoured cars, lorries, guns of various kinds; its stocks of ammunition in different categories and of fuels; its battle casualties in killed and wounded; its material losses, differentiated between complete write-offs, machines repairable by the unit within 24 hours,

[1]In Morse W/T all figures are spelled out in words. So a message like this took longer to transmit than would appear at first sight. This could be material if our D/F stations were taking a fix on the German transmitters at that moment.

others repairable only at rear workshops. Sometimes a separate message would show that an increase from, say, 27 to 33 in a certain paragraph from one day to the next could be accounted for by the reported arrival of 6 new armoured cars.

Some of these pro formas were long and complex. Not all units used the same forms. But gradually the key to each could be reconstructed and the information in the daily reports could then be conveyed exactly to the British commanders facing the units whose strengths and weaknesses were thereby revealed. It was — to cite an obvious example — of the utmost value to know that a certain German tank regiment had a reasonably full complement of tanks but no petrol to put into them. Because of their importance I give at the end of this book some examples of these daily returns.

In addition to routine tactical intelligence of this nature North African Ultra yielded an unusual number of high level exchanges. I remember no other context where Hitler's personal signature, normally a rarity, appeared more frequently. One reason was Rommel's relative inaccessibility on the other side of the Mediterranean which made communication by radio imperative; neither telephone nor couriers would serve. Another reason was the Italian involvement and the resulting diplomatic discussion of grand strategy and the shared high command. In Rome, which became a halfway house between the German High Command and Panzer Army Africa, Hitler stationed a Supreme Commander (Kesselring) over all his army and air forces in the Mediterranean and also a special section for liaison between Panzer Army Africa and the Italian Comando Supremo. Some of the resulting correspondence was highly interesting.

For example, in the afternoon of 2 November 1942, in a message which was decyphered at BP at about 5 a.m. the following morning, Rommel sent to Kesselring, to Comando Supremo and to the highest military quarters in Germany a stark appreciation in which he forecast the annihilation of his armies. This was a few days after his defeat by Montgomery at Alamein. These were his words:

> After ten days of the hardest fighting against the British who are many times superior on land and in the air and in spite of the defensive success today, the strength of the army is

exhausted. The army will therefore no longer be in a position to prevent a further attempt by strong enemy tank formations to break through which may be expected tonight or tomorrow. An ordered withdrawal of the 6 Italian and 2 German non-motorized divisions or brigades is not possible in view of the lack of M/T vehicles. A large part of these units will probably fall into the hands of the fully motorized enemy. But also the mobile troops are so intricately involved in the battle that only a part of them will be able to extricate themselves from the enemy. The slight stocks of fuel do not allow of a movement to the rear over great distances. On the one available road the army will certainly be attacked day and night by the RAF. In this situation, in spite of the heroic resistance and the excellent spirit of the troops the possibility of the gradual annihilation of the army must be faced.

Rommel got a victory-or-death reply from the Führer and after further exchanges the Luftwaffe in Africa received a withering blast from Goering who told them that they had lost their honour and had become the objects of the bitterest scorn of their comrades on the eastern and Channel fronts.

Rommel escaped annihilation for the time being. He retreated westward, unable to join battle again and pursued at a distance by Montgomery's 8 Army. In the same month of November and far to the west of his defeated forces a mixed allied force under General Dwight D Eisenhower was put ashore in Morocco and Algeria — but not Tunisia. Rommel was now between two fires. He was also ill, as we knew from reading a long report on his health from a senior army doctor. Rommel told Hitler that he would probably be unable to remain in commmand after he had got his army back to the Mareth line between Tripolitania and Tunisia. All this we knew from Ultra.

Hitler's riposte to the allied landings in Morocco and Algeria was to put an army into Tunisia. Its first commander, General Walter Nehring, took such a dim view of his prospects that he had to be removed after a few weeks; his successor, General Friedemund von Arnim, did not assess the situation very differently but held on for six months — partly because of the steel will of his superior in Rome, Kesselring, and also because of his own training as an officer in the old conservative

Prussian tradition which avoided asking questions unlikely to get acceptable answers.

There were on the German side two views about the appropriate function of Arnim's army. Hitler's was simple and emphatic. He planned a junction between Arnim and Rommel in order that their combined forces might preserve the German-Italian presence in Africa indefinitely. The opposing view was that the point of seizing the Tunisian bridge-head was to enable Rommel's forces to pass through it back into Europe. The passage between Tunisia and Sicily was the shortest way across the Mediterranean and all others were too risky.

But whichever strategy was to prevail something had to be done about the twin threat posed by Eisenhower's forces pressing into Tunisia from Algeria and Montgomery's army approaching from the opposite quarter. Arnim and Rommel joined forces in Tunisia at the end of January and proceeded to make a series of poorly co-ordinated attacks to the west. Their success was modest, for although Rommel gave the Americans a bloody nose at the Kasserine pass, no part of Eisenhower's forces was obliged to retreat far and Rommel had to break off and face about in order to confront Montgomery advancing menacingly from Tripolitania into Tunisia. Ultra then played Rommel a dirty trick.

Hitler, on somewhat fanciful grounds, had ordered Rommel to face Montgomery at the Mareth line, an old defensive position constructed by the French in an earlier generation to protect themselves against the Italians in Tripolitania. The line was long, ill-equipped and without any natural protection at its western end. Rommel preferred a line further north which was both shorter and protected to the west by difficult terrain, but Hitler would not hear of it, apparently because it was beyond the border between the two territories and so smacked of the abandonment of a part of Tunisia. So Rommel planned to swing back from Kasserine south-eastward to the Mareth line and there ambush Montgomery's advance guard before the main body of 8 Army could reach it. Montgomery's forces were tenuously strung out and Rommel hoped to deal him a blow which would yet again reverse the pendulum of the desert war and send him reeling back towards Egypt.

Rommel duly explained his intentions to Kesselring over the water in Rome. Within hours BP had read his plan and conveyed it to Montgomery. Ordered into full speed ahead Montgomery's main body arrived next morning in time to defeat Rommel who left Africa two days later never to return. Surviving German documents show that Rommel realized that his plan must have been betrayed to his enemy, but he did not know what had taken the vital element of surprise out of it. We shall come later to the Germans' exaggerated faith in the security of their cyphers.

*

We turn from Africa to the Atlantic and to the most dangerous of all Hitler's operations in the west after the Battle of Britain. The Battle of the Atlantic is the battle which Hitler could have won and nearly won, but which he lost because of Ultra.

BP's first break of naval Enigma was made on 12 March 1941. The message had been originated by a U-boat in the very early hours of 27 February (0122 hours German time). It was addressed to the Commander-in-Chief of U-boats and it read:

No D/F Vs yet received from U97.

Somewhat more promising from the intelligence point of view was another message originated in the evening of 27 February and also decyphered at BP on 12 March:

Naval attaché Washington reports convoy rendezvous 25 February 200 sea miles east of Sable island 13 cargo boats 4 tankers 100,000 tons cargo aeroplane parts machine parts motor lorries munitions chemicals probably the number of the convoy is HX 114.

Such were the beginnings of BP's invasion of naval Enigma. On that first day seven messages were decyphered and relayed to the Admiralty, all of them originated on 26 or 27 February, i.e. two weeks earlier. On the next two days, 13 and 14 March, the number of decodes rose to thirteen and fourteen respectively, all of messages originated on 27 or 28 February. Business was not very brisk but it was beginning to become regular. By the end of the year 25,000 naval Enigma messages had been read. 1942 yielded 72,000. When in May 1945 all naval Enigma machines fell silent about half a million of their messages had been read at BP and in the Admiralty.[1]

The German navy used many Enigma cyphers. Some of them were never read at all, chiefly because they carried an inadequate volume of traffic: for example, the special cyphers used by the pocket battleships and the armed merchant cruisers. But the main operational naval cypher, called Hydra, was broken continuously, although with varying time lags, from March 1941 to the end of the war. It was the cypher used by surface ships (and up to February 1942 by U-boats) in the Atlantic, North Sea and coastal waters of occupied countries outside the Mediterranean.

The first break was helped by a series of lucky and planned captures. In February 1941 the raid on the Lofoten Islands off the Norwegian coast in the Arctic circle produced an unexpected bonus in the shape of some spare Enigma wheels. A few months later cypher books were recovered from two weather reporting ships, the *München* and the *Lauenburg*, which were captured for this very purpose. Between these two captures, in fact two days after the capture of the *München* at the beginning of May, U-110 was put out of action on the surface and abandoned but not scuttled by her crew. U-110 yielded a naval Enigma machine. It seems likely that the death of U-110's Captain Lemp occurred when, realizing the danger of allowing her papers and her Enigma to fall into enemy hands, he tried unsuccessfully to regain his ship to scuttle her and so drowned. These captures clinched the work of Hut 8 at BP and so hastened the breaking not only of Hydra but also of other naval cyphers, including those used by U-boats and surface ships (Medusa and Süd) in the Mediterranean and Black Sea.

The Battle of the Atlantic falls, from the Ultra point of view, into four stages. In the first, up to mid-1941, we had the merest sniff of naval Ultra but we had Luftwaffe Ultra which sometimes contributed to the picture of the war on the ocean. In the second stage, we had Hydra but in February 1942 the

[1]It is still impossible to give the precise figure. The number in the Public Record Office is 388,188, stretching from 13 March 1941 to the end of the war; but this total excludes the U-boat traffic after December 1942 which constitutes a separate series not yet transferred to the PRO.

General Guderian and a two-man Enigma team. The man in the middle
is the keyboard operator. His colleague will take down the letters
which show up on the plate behind the keys.

The Château de Vignolles, France

The pre-war BBC Television transmitter at Alexandra Palace in North London which was used to jam Y-Gerät

# VIII. Beispiel.

17 Gültiger Tagesschlüssel:

(Ausschnitt aus der für die Verschlüsselung des Klartextes
in Betracht kommenden Schlüsseltafel, z. B. , . . . . . . . . . .
Maschinenschlüssel für Monat Mai.)

| Datum | Walzenlage | Ringstellung | Grundstellung |
|---|---|---|---|
| 4. | I III II | 16  11  13 | 01  12  22 |

| Steckerverbindung | Kenngruppen-Einsaßstelle . . . . . . Gruppe | Kenngruppen |
|---|---|---|
| CO DI FR HU JW LS TX | 2 | adq nuz opw vxz |

Nach diesem Tagesschlüssel ist die Chiffriermaschine einzustellen (vgl.
Ziff. 4 und 5).

Der im nachfolgenden Beispiel eingesetzte Schlüsseltext ist aus Geheim-
haltungsgründen nicht mit der Chiffriermaschine getastet, sondern willkürlich
gewählt worden.

## A. Verschlüsseln.

18. Zu verschlüsselnder Spruch:

Tag 4. 5.,

Abgangzeit 17,55 Uhr

Korpskommando VI

angreift 5. Mai 0345 Uhr mit 3. und 10. Div. Feind bei Maisach.
Gef. Stand: Milbertshofen Nordausgang

19. Für die Verschlüsselung ist der Klartext des Spruches gem. H. Dv. g. 7,
Ziff. 40 wie folgt niederzuschreiben:

Korpskommando roem x  seqs  angreift fuenften mai null drei
vier fuenf uhr mit dritter und zehnter div x feind bei maisach x
gef stand x milbertshofen nordausgang

20. Auf dem Spruchformular bezeichnet der Schlüßler die im Tagesschlüssel vorgeschriebene Einsaßstelle (im Beispiel 2. Gruppe) für die Kenn-
gruppe und spart diese Gruppe beim Eintragen des Spruchschlüssels bzw.
des Schlüsseltextes aus.

A page from the Enigma users' manual

```
TO I D 8 G                        ZTP/1054

FROM GERMAN NAVAL SECTION G C AND C S


110/4595 KC/S                          TOI 0025/27/5/41
                    TOO 0153

TO  FLEET W 70

ENEMY REPORT:

TO C IN C AFLOAT:

I THANK YOU IN THE NAME OF THE ENTIRE GERMAN PEOPLE.  ADOLF
HITLER
TO THE CREW OF THE BATTLESHIP BISMARCK:

ALL GERMANY IS WITH YOU.  ALL THAT CAN STILL BE DONE, WILL BE
DONE,  YOUR DEVOTION TO DUTY WILL FORTIFY OUR PEOPLE IN THEIR
STRUGGLE FOR EXISTENCE.  ADOLF HITLER.


TOO 2229/29/5/41+++AGT+++
```

Two German signals transmitted before and after the sinking of the
*Bismarck*. These are the verbatim translations sent to the Admiralty by
BP's Naval Section — which sent about 500,000 such teleprints in the
course of the war. Hitler's thanks to Admiral Lütjens and his doomed
crew (above) were transmitted on 27 May 1941, 25 minutes after
midnight and ten hours before the *Bismarck* went down. The grisly
inquiry (below) was made shortly after midday on the 28th. Neither
message was read at BP until the 29th

```
TO I D 8 G                        ZTP/1032

FROM GERMAN NAVAL SECTION G C AND C S



12040 KC/S                             TOI 1217/28/5/41
                    TOO 1400

FROM SACHSENWALD

ARE BODIES TO BE FISHED UP?


TOO 2059/29/5/41+++AGT+++
```

REF: CX/MSS/T349/82                    HP 4646

ZZZZZ

((HP 4646 £ 4646 CR ONA ON QX YKA YK GU 9 £ 9 TG. 86 £ 86

WM 52 £ 52 NX 35 £ 35 LF 45 £ 45 AD 19 £ 19 EFR 41 £ 41

SH 70 £ 70 %


ORDERS AT TWO ONE FOUR NOUGHT HOURS TWENTYSIXTH FOR

TWENTYSEVENTH.  FIRSTLY, FIRST GRUPPE KING FIVE ONE)) TO

ATTACK EINDHOVEN £ EINDHOVEN TOWN EXCLUSIVELY ON

TWENTYSEVENTH IN SUPPORT OF GERMAN TANK ATTACK ON IN

EINDHOVEN £ EINDHOVEN AREA.  SECONDLY, ALTERNATIVE TARGETS

(ABLE) CROSSINGS NEAR NIJMEGEN £ NIJMEGEN (BAKER)

HERTOGENBOSCH £ HERTOGENBOSCH.  THIRDLY, ALTERNATIVE

TARGETS TO BE ATTACKED ONLY IF ATTACK ON MAIN TARGET NOT

£ NOT POSSIBLE OWING WEATHER



NH                              270134Z/10/44

GB

An urgent signal from Hut 3 to 11 commands overseas giving German
orders for bombing operations on the following day. The German
orders were issued at 2140 hours on 26 October 1944. They must have
been decyphered within about 3 hours, since Hut 3's signal was sent at
0134 hours on the 27th. This is one of about 100,000 signals from Hut
3 to commands. The CX/MSS reference at the top refers to the
verbatim translation of the German original teleprinted to London. The
number of Zs (from one to five) indicates the message's priority on BP's
own signals network — the SLUs. The letters and numbers preceding
the text show to whom it was sent. The initials at the foot are those of
the Adviser (army or air) who drafted the signal and of the Hut 3 Duty
Officer who approved it

A message being received by radio: encoded Enigma messages were sent in morse

The Colossus, the world's first electronic computer, created by BP mathematicians and Post Office engineers. It helped with the decyphering of Enigma but was designed primarily to deal with what might come after Enigma

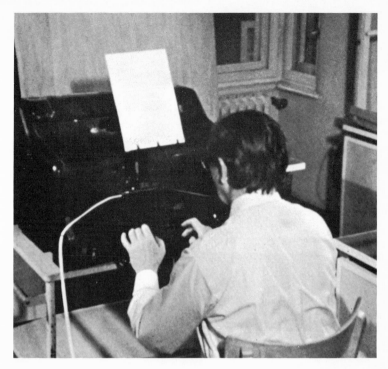

The Geheimschreiber. This machine, much more complex and ponderous than Enigma, was used only at the highest levels. Towards the end of the war BP feared that it was coming into more general use — and that would almost certainly have been the end of Ultra

Three of the ten wheels of the Geheimschreiber

The author in 1942

U-boats stopped using Hydra and we became blind to their activities so far as Ultra was concerned. This situation persisted during the third stage, the menacing months of February to December 1942. Finally, in December 1942 we broke the new Atlantic U-boat cypher Triton.

One of the most thrilling episodes of the war in the Atlantic occurred just within the first stage. This was the nine days of active life of the battleship *Bismarck*.

The *Bismarck* sailed on 18 May 1941 from the Baltic port of Gdynia on what was to be her first and last voyage. She was accompanied by the cruiser *Prinz Eugen* and commanded by Admiral Lütjens. Six days out from Gdynia she sank the veteran British cruiser *Hood* and three days later she was herself at the bottom of the sea just outside the zone of safety for which she was making off the west coast of France.

From the time she had been commissioned in August 1940 the *Bismarck* had been watched with anxious attention by the Admiralty, chiefly by air reconnaissance and traffic analysis. Surface raiders had done terrible damage to shipping in the Atlantic. While the *Bismarck* completed her trials the battle cruisers *Scharnhorst* and *Gneisenau*, which had already had two punishing cruises in the Atlantic, were waiting at Brest and might be ordered back to sea in conjunction with a sortie by the *Bismarck*. The resulting havoc could cripple Britain.

The *Bismarck*'s exit from the Baltic was preceded by intense German air reconnaissance all the way from Norway to Iceland and Greenland and this activity was both reflected in the volume of low-grade cypher traffic measured by the Y service and reported by Ultra. Clearly it presaged a major event. Then the passage of an unidentified battleship up the Norwegian coast was reported by a Swedish ship which happened to sight her indistinctly and by a resistance group in Norway, and both reports quickly reached London. They were confirmed by photographic reconnaissance which removed all doubt about her identity. The *Bismarck* was on the high seas and making for the Atlantic.

The immediate question was whether she would attempt the passage between the Faroes and Iceland or take the longer route north of Iceland and then through the Denmark Strait between Iceland and Greenland. A British squadron with the *Prince of Wales* and *Hood* was at once despatched to intercept

87

her in the Denmark Strait. Another, with the Commander-in-Chief of the Home Fleet, Admiral Sir Francis Tovey, in the *King George V* moved shortly afterwards from Scapa Flow to positions south of Iceland.

In the fading light of 23 May the *Bismarck* was sighted by the cruiser *Suffolk* and at 0600 the next morning she ran unexpectedly into the *Hood* and *Prince of Wales*. She sank the *Hood* and crippled the *Prince of Wales*. Later that day the second British squadron made contact and scored a hit on the *Bismarck* with aircraft from the carrier *Victorious*. At this point Admiral Lütjens, perhaps because he was afraid of running short of fuel, decided to part company with the *Prinz Eugen* and make for Brest. This was at 1800 on the 24th. By 0306 on the 25th the British forces had lost *Bismarck*.

Twenty-seven hours after sinking the *Hood* Lütjens did an extraordinarily foolhardy thing. Beginning at 0852 on the 25th he sent to Germany a signal whose transmission took half an hour. The interception of this message was virtually certain to give away his position by D/F and he must therefore have believed that he was still being shadowed, which he was not. Yet he nearly got away with it. His transmission was intercepted and gave bearings on his position not only from stations in Britain but also Iceland and Gibraltar. The bearings were repeated by the Admiralty to Tovey but they were wrongly interpreted in the *King George V*. As a result of this mistake Tovey believed that the *Bismarck*'s course was not east, as was the case, but north-east. For the best part of the day Tovey's squadron steamed in the wrong direction on the assumption that his quarry was making for northern waters and not for France.

That France was her destination was by now established with increasing certainty in the Admiralty. Traffic analysis showed a sharp rise in wireless activity in the Brest area, pointing to the imminence of an exceptional event. Ultra made its contribution by disclosing preparations by the Luftwaffe to provide cover for an unspecified purpose which seemed, in the general context, to be likely to be the shielding of the *Bismarck*. The Admiralty, at a loss to understand Tovey's interpretation of the situation but convinced that it must be wrong, initiated air reconnaissance over the approaches to Brest where, at 1030 on the 26th, a Catalina of Coastal

Command sighted the *Bismarck*. This sighting was the first event in the last act of the drama. It was effected by a combination of three kinds of intelligence: D/F, traffic analysis and Ultra.

A third British naval force, which included the aircraft carrier *Ark Royal*, was making all possible speed northwards from Gibraltar and at dusk on the 26th a lucky hit by an aircraft of the *Ark Royal* on *Bismarck*'s propellers and rudders slowed her down and forced her for a while to go round in circles. After a further air attack the next morning she became a sitting target waiting for Tovey's ships to come up and sink her. This they did at 1036 on the 27th.

During this last night Lütjens had no doubt what his fate was to be. At last light on the 26th, using his naval Enigma cyphers, he sent three short messages reporting that he had been attacked from the air and hit by torpedoes astern and amidships. Shortly afterwards he signalled to Grand Admiral Raeder: 'Ship unmanageable. We shall fight to the last shell. Long live the Führer.' In the closing minutes of the day he sent two more signals. The first was addressed to 'The Führer of the German Reich Adolf Hitler' and was marked urgent: 'We shall fight to the end thinking of you and confident as a rock in the victory of Germany.' One minute later came the sombre report: 'Ship's guns and engines are absolutely intact. However she will not steer on the engines.' But none of these messages was decyphered at BP until the 28th, by which time the *Bismarck* had gone down.

In these dramatic nine days the lives and deaths of thousands of men and the fate of great ships were swayed by extraordinary errors. Admiral Lütjens all but doomed his ship when he transmitted his long message the morning after sinking the *Hood*. The confusion over the D/F bearings of this message all but allowed the *Bismarck* to reach the safety of French coastal waters: she would have escaped Tovey's final bombardment had she not been maimed by the *Ark Royal*. And in the closing stages Ultra made a second contribution to the tale.

In these days an important German personage happened to be in Athens — General Hans Jeschonnek, the Chief of Staff of the Luftwaffe. He had a special reason for wanting to know what was going on. It has been conjectured that he had a son or other close relative in the *Bismarck*, which was in fact carrying

89

a number of young naval cadets. (But Jeschonnek had no son.) Berlin had of course received Lütjens's long signal of the 25th, but it was not read at BP. Then in response to the inquiries from Athens, Berlin repeated the message to Athens — in a Luftwaffe cypher which BP did read.

Because of its length the signal was sent in two parts which, for cyphering and decyphering purposes, counted as two separate messages. As soon as the first of these began to be read in Hut 6 its crucial importance was obvious. But it ended without divulging the position or course of the *Bismarck*. These, it appeared more than probable, would come in the second part which must be lying in the pile of traffic for that day which was waiting to be decyphered. It was quickly spotted. To the amazement and dismay of all concerned it would not come out. The settings were known and there should have been no problems. It dawned on the baffled cryptographers in Hut 6 that they were stuck because the German operator had himself made a mistake. They then had the task of trying to imagine what sort of mistake they might have made if they had been in that operator's position. They succeeded. The second part of the message finally revealed itself and in it were the position and course of the *Bismarck*.

So Ultra, at a critical moment, provided the Admiralty with most welcome confirmation of the assumption upon which it was directing the search for the *Bismarck*. It placed beyond doubt the Admiralty view that Tovey was on the wrong tack and that the German ship, far from being away to the north, was making for and had a good chance of reaching Brest.

*

From 1 June, five days after the *Bismarck* went down, naval Ultra became copious. With its help most of the tankers and other ancillary vessels which had put to sea to service the *Bismarck* and the *Prinz Eugen* were tracked down and sunk.

After the sinking of the *Bismarck* no fresh threat to Atlantic shipping from German capital ships ever materialized but the far more serious threat by U-boats persisted and grew worse. 1942 was a bad year for the allies. In February the Atlantic U-boats stopped using Hydra which we had been reading for nearly a year and were given a special new cypher of their own — Triton. The first consequence of the introduction of Triton was to wipe out, as far as BP was concerned, the traffic of the one German arm which might still win the war in the west for Hitler, and this increasingly alarming state of affairs continued for ten months. But in December Triton broke. This was Ultra's greatest triumph. Thereafter Triton was read regularly, although not always without delays: delays of one day to a week were not uncommon. The gravest scare occurred in March 1943 as a result of the introduction of the fourth wheel for the naval Enigma machine. BP, which was forewarned and on the lookout for the change, warned the Admiralty that the traffic might be lost for months but the problems were surmounted in ten days. March 1943 was the last month to see a major German U-boat victory in the Atlantic.

In 1941 1,299 vessels sailing the Atlantic on British account had been lost — a gross tonnage of 4.3 million. In 1942 the tonnage lost rose by 80 per cent, to 7.8 million. During that year the U-boat fleet rose from under 100 to over 200 and Admiral Doenitz was keeping 100 boats at sea at a time; four out of every five vessels sunk by the Germans were sunk by U-boats. Doenitz believed that he could win the war for Germany by sinking 800,000 tons of shipping a month and in 1942 he exceeded that target three times. Significantly, the last time that he did so was November 1942, the month before the breaking of Triton. Then in 1943 he was forced for a time to withdraw all his boats from the North Atlantic. In the last week of May they were ordered to retreat to south-west of the Azores. Improved radar and a new type of depth-charge accounted in part for this swing of fortune but the outstanding cause was the reading of the U-boat cypher. Ultra enabled the Admiralty to play hide-and-seek in the Atlantic with its eyes open. As a U-boat or pack of U-boats was ordered to move to a position across the path of a convoy, that convoy's route was deflected to the north or south to outflank the waiting enemy, while U-boat chasers were directed to the spot where they could make a kill. It was a breath-taking contest directed from an underground headquarters in London but enacted in the murderous waters and winds of the ocean.

The Germans resisted the idea that their naval Enigma might be insecure. They ascribed their mounting U-boat losses to improvements in D/F techniques and new kinds of radar. Yet the German Admiralty should have been the first to suspect the real source of its misfortunes since it had itself been reading British naval cyphers, including the British convoy cypher. So long as it did so, it too played the game of moving pieces about the ocean to counter moves by the other side, but as British cypher security became more rigorous the German crypto-graphers lost their way. There are two excellent books about this deadly game: *Very Special Intelligence* by Patrick Beesly and *Convoy Battles in 1943* by Jürgen Rohwer. During the war Beesly served in the Admiralty's Operational Intelligence Centre, Rohwer in a German U-boat.

*

The winter of 1942-43 was also the winter of Stalingrad. What did we tell our Russian allies about Ultra and what did Ultra tell us about Hitler's intentions and campaigns against the USSR?

Hitler's first directive for the invasion of the USSR was issued on 18 December 1940 and the invasion began on 22 June 1941. Until almost the last moment there was strong resistance in London to believing that Hitler would do any such thing. There were various reasons for this tenacious belief in spite of a good deal of evidence to the contrary. The shock of the Russo-German pact of 1939 was still fresh and many people found it difficult to suppose that so spectacular a deal should be undone in two years. Napoleon's disastrous incursion in 1812, one of the most famous episodes in European history, suggested that Hitler would steer clear of a comparable blunder. And in the tense and claustrophobic atmosphere of 1940-41, when Britain was Hitler's sole fighting enemy, London was far more inclined to debate where Hitler would strike the British empire next rather than whether or not he might strike somebody else first. Once the German invasion of the British Isles had been frustrated, it became the business of planning and intelligence staffs to worry about British imperial positions in the Middle East and Asia; and in doing so they were much readier to foresee a Russo-German agreement for the partition of the British empire — a sequel to the partition of Poland — than a Russo-German war.

Yet the evidence was otherwise. *Mein Kampf*, amid a good deal that was discursive and obscure, contained two clear themes: Germany's need to conquer *Lebensraum* at Russian expense and mankind's need to exterminate the Jews. More persuasive by 1940-41 were the rumours and reports, gradually turning into hard evidence, of Hitler's immediate intentions. Churchill's first warning to Stalin was delivered in mid-1940, and during the first months of 1941 there could be no gainsaying the German military build-up, although there were still disputes in London about its purpose; it was interpreted by some as a threat to be used against Stalin in forthcoming bargaining for a new Russo-German pact. Churchill, however, was sufficiently impressed by the evidence to repeat his warnings, which were now reaching Stalin from many other quarters as well. But what Stalin might be thinking or doing in this situation was very imperfectly known since not only was he not telling, but we had lost our penetration of Russian cyphers fifteen years earlier — in 1926 when Baldwin, speaking in the debate in the House of Commons on the Arcos raid, had unwittingly quoted a Russian decode *verbatim* and so given the game away.

The most convincing volume of evidence about Hitler's plans for 1941 came from signals intelligence and Ultra. I have already described how the monitoring of undecyphered wireless traffic disclosed the movements of Luftwaffe units to eastern Poland, and this intelligence was supplemented by Ultra which reported a massive shift of both air and ground forces from the western and Balkan fronts to the Russian front. Even the German Army's General Staff was transferred from Berlin eastward, a fact which we knew from Ultra before the beginning of 1941.

German wireless traffic on the eastern fronts was more difficult to intercept than western or Mediterranean traffic for simple geographical reasons. But we heard and decyphered a great deal. Initially, when it seemed as though the USSR might be defeated in a matter of weeks or months, there was a natural reluctance to convey Ultra intelligence to Stalin but once it became clear that the USSR would not be knocked out of the war at a stroke, both loyalty and expediency required us to give the Russians everything that might help them to resist and then defeat the Germans. The provision of intelligence could be as crucial as the supply of tanks and fuel, boots and telephone cable.

There was never any question of divulging the Ultra secret: the fact that we were able to read German high-grade cyphers. Russian signals security was very bad and the Germans read a good deal of Russian traffic, as we knew from reading German traffic. That being so, to tell the Russians that we were reading Enigma would be tantamount to telling the Germans too.

Equally, however, there was no question of not conveying to Moscow a substantial amount of intelligence, including intelligence derived from Ultra so far as this could be done without imperilling the source. In practice this meant deciding how much should be imparted and how.

The answer to the second question was straightforward. Attached to the British military mission in Moscow was a single officer — Major Crankshaw, already mentioned — who represented BP, Broadway, Military Intelligence and also the Admiralty. He was a complex node of intelligence in his own person and he reported to the ambassador who in turn passed on personally to Stalin whatever secret intelligence London decided to vouchsafe. How much was conveyed varied with circumstances. In general Churchill himself, while he never considered telling Stalin whence Ultra came, was temperamentally in favour of giving more information rather than less. He was not the only one in this frame of mind, but he had on occasions to be restrained by others who feared that he was taking too many risks.

In sum a considerable amount of intelligence was passed to the Russians. We do not know whether they guessed where it came from. If they did not, then they were of course ignorant of the peculiar authenticity of what they were being told. In the case of the great tank battles of 1942, for example, when they were warned that they were pouring men and materials into a huge German trap, it is difficult to suppose that they gave full credence to warnings which, if headed, would have saved them terrible losses.

If on the other hand they did guess that we had a very special source which we were unwilling to share with them, what did they make of that? They must have captured Enigma machines and cypher books and they must have supposed that we did so too. They were not lacking in mathematicians and chess-players capable of appreciating what was involved in breaking the cyphers. They may themselves have been without an organization like BP capable of making the most of such skills, but it would have been natural for them to harbour at least a suspicion that we possessed a precious advantage which we were withholding from them. They were certainly suspicious in general, often unfairly. Yet neither directly nor indirectly did they probe Eden or anybody else on the subject of Ultra.

There is a further unanswerable question. How far did the intelligence imbalance affect the way the war ended and so the relative geographical positions of the western and eastern allies when the Germans surrendered? If Ultra's contribution to the Battle of the Atlantic hastened 'Overlord', and if 'Overlord' itself and the subsequent campaigns of 1944-45 were materially assisted by Ultra, it can be argued that Ultra enabled the western allies to get to the middle of Germany before confronting the Russians, whereas in the absence of Ultra this meeting might have taken place on the Rhine instead of the Elbe. The post-war map of Europe would have looked very different if the Russians had occupied the whole of Germany on their own and had met their allies on a line running from Antwerp to Strasbourg. Equally, however, it can be argued that the Russian advance would have been slower if the Germans had not been forced by critical pressures in the west, for which Ultra was partly responsible, to detach ground and air forces from their eastern fronts to meet the successful allied invasion of France and the reconquest of western Europe. These unhistorical reflections deserve a glance, if no more.

After Hitler's invasion of the USSR Churchill directed BP to stop working on Russian cyphers.

*

Before the spring of 1943 turned into summer the war, although far from over, was won and lost. The tide was now running against Hitler and in order to reverse it he needed something akin to a miracle — an inexplicable Russian collapse, a radically improved kind of U-boat, V-weapons against which there could be no defence. But he got none.

My purpose in this book is not to rewrite the history of the war with Ultra thrown in but to give some account of what Ultra was, how it was got and what its uses were. I have tried to illustrate the nature and the uses of Ultra with particular reference to the mid-war campaigns of 1942-43. Generally speaking Ultra provided in the ensuing two years more of the same. The volume never flagged until the total collapse of the German war machine. In the calender year 1944 Hut 3's signals to commands numbered 44,000 — well over 100 a day. At BP the increase in volume and its application to new battles kept us all on our toes, while to its recipients in the field Ultra became an established, expected part of the picture. Planning and operations staffs became familiar with the kind of material that Ultra provided, and in consequence Ultra influenced planning in ways which the planners themselves may not have fully realized. 'Overlord' — the allied landings in Normandy in June 1944 — provides the best example.

The decision where to land in France was a hard one. The crossing from Kent to the Pas de Calais was shorter and easier to defend from the air, besides being nearer to Germany where everybody felt that the war must end. The crossing to Normandy was more hazardous in more ways than one and the decision to go that way would make little sense except upon the assumption that the Germans could be deceived into believing that there would be massive landings elsewhere too. Totally to deceive the Germans about the choice of Normandy never seemed feasible, but they might be led to suppose that Normandy was not the main point of invasion, or not the only one. The aim was to tie down as many German divisions as possible as far as possible from Normandy for as long as possible. Failure to do this would allow Hitler to concentrate all his available forces in the vital area and so to make the invasion not only much more costly but probably a failure. In the event the Anglo-American deception plans were a huge success and Ultra played a significant, perhaps vital, part in them.

There were three prerequisites for the success of the invasion: command of the sea, command of the air, and the dispersal of the German ground forces. Without any one of these it would be all but impossible to achieve the dual purpose of getting and holding the beach-heads, and of doing so with the minimum of casualties. Command of the sea and of the air was assured before the expedition sailed. The bombing of communications helped to hamper reinforcement. But the main element in weakening the German opposition was the creation of a number of unreal threats, some peripheral and one central. The peripheral threats, mainly to the German positions in Norway and Denmark, were created by the simulation of large but non-existent forces in Scotland waiting to invade Scandinavia. The central threat was posed by the creation of an even larger body of non-existent troops in East Anglia and south-east England, destined to be carried into the Pas de Calais some weeks after the invasion of Normandy, which in this cover plan was made to appear a subsidiary part of a wider developing strategy.

This complex deception depended on the use of double agents and Ultra. BP had been reading the Enigma traffic of the German secret service (the Abwehr) since 1941. It thus helped British counter-intelligence to pick up German agents and turn them into double agents, who were then used to plant false information on the Abwehr. Ultra then revealed how far the Abwehr was swallowing the bait and which agents it was continuing to believe in. The use and monitoring of agents in this way supplemented the deceptive wireless spoof which simulated the existence of armies which were not there; in at least one case a false report sent in the name of an agent still trusted by the Abwehr caused the cancellation of an order to move a whole German army (15 Army) to Normandy. In the same way Ultra helped to create in the German mind an entirely phoney British army in Egypt in 1944 and to magnify the strengths of two other armies in the Mediterranean and give them aggressive intentions which they never had or could have had.

The volume of BP's service to overseas commands after D-day may be illustrated by a figure which I have picked from the records at random. In the period from 0033 hours on 20 July to 0017 hours on 22 July — a stretch of 48 hours — Hut 3 despatched 250 signals. Not all of these related to the fronts in France, for Hut 3 was at this time handling a great deal of detailed traffic about operations in Italy and also about shipping movements in the Aegean and the Adriatic. On the western fronts, besides the stream of order of battle material of which I give examples in Appendix Two, Ultra provided

97

requests and orders by German units for reconnaissance; reports on the ensuing operations and the deductions drawn by the Germans from them; the front line and other reports on the day's fighting and German appreciations of allied intentions. For example, the Panzer Lehr Division 'appreciated ... evening 19th that allied reconnaissance pointed to large scale attack in division's sector 20th.' This was relayed to allied commanders at 0221 hours on the 20th. More generally, Ultra revealed in the ensuing months the nature of Hitler's plans to stem the allied advance. As landlines became increasingly disrupted more traffic was thrown onto the air, including messages of exhortation and threats from Hitler himself as well as information on supplies, reinforcements and the areas of operation of the German ground and air forces, unit by unit — all of which played a part in the debates at Eisenhower's headquarters about the best way to end the war as quickly as possible. Ultra also gave a fairly full, and ominously disquieting, picture of the German forces available to move against the Arnhem parachute operation in September. In retrospect it is sobering to see that the doubts cast by Ultra over this venture were felt also by intelligence officers at lower levels who had no knowledge of Ultra and were somewhat roughly treated for expressing their reservations.

Interspersed with this more or less regular service came items of a more general nature. At the end of July:

Meindl[1] on 20th felt it his duty to call attention to fact that fighting power of paratroops was steadily sinking and that the utmost demands made of them had been exceeded. His two requests for provision of replacements had so far remained unanswered. On account of the critical situation last replacements had had to be employed on the most arduous operations at once. Result was that as was always the case ninety per cent became casualties within a few days. Responsibility could not be accepted for sending these young untrained replacements (who, if trained, might give an excellent account of themselves and who were an élite body of men both as regards physique and fighting spirit) against the enemy in such conditions. Majority had never

[1]Meindl was a parachute general.

yet thrown a live hand grenade. Thirty per cent had so far
only fired 5-10 rounds of live ammunition. Scarcely any had
been trained in MGs, to say nothing of use of entrenching
tools and camouflage. This state of affairs was to be attributed to negligence of training regiments in respect of
equipment and provision of cadre personnel.

Two months later came this note of desperation from the Commander-in-Chief West himself:

Von Rundstedt order of 16th September emphasized that
the fight on German soil must increase German fanaticism.
Every pillbox, block of houses or village to be defended
until allies bled to death or garrison dead. No longer
question of operations on grand scale, only task to hold
positions or be annihilated. Commanders to ensure that this
fanaticism continually increased in troops and civilians and
effectively used as a weapon against interlopers on German
soil. Anyone, officer or man, apathetic and unaware of
decisive responsiblity of the hour and who did not carry out
task with complete disregard for his life to be removed and
proceedings taken against him. All authorities to ensure, by
applying comprehensive and draconian methods, that the
will to resist in the troops was re-established and main-
tained.

In the last year of the war in Europe political and merely
personal matters crept into the Enigma traffic alongside the
tactical and strategic. In the early hours of 21 July Ultra
revealed the special orders issued by Hitler immediately after
the failure to assassinate him the day before. It also produced
the conspirators' proclamation to key posts which began with
the words: 'The Führer is dead.' Ominously this transmission
broke off before the end. One of Hitler's decisions was to
confer even more power and authority on Himmler. Yet two
days later Himmler was finding time for something very
different from his multifarious public duties. In a message
beginning 'Dear Wolfling' and addressed to his friend and
chief subordinate in Italy, SS General Karl Wolff, Himmler
urged Wolff to get hold of as many Florentine works of art as
possible. In August General Count Alexander Neubronn von
Eisenburg, who had the job of managing Pétain in Vichy,

reported that the Marshal was refusing to go on being managed. He asked for fresh instructions but before he received them he had to report that Pétain had asked him to leave Vichy on the grounds that his mission had come to an end. In September General Hermann Ramcke, once a dashing parachute leader but now marooned in the Atlantic fortress of Brest as the fighting faded far away to the east, appealed to Hitler to help his children. In a direct appeal to the Führer he begged:

> I have not been able to carry out my plan to purchase a home on my ancestral soil from the proceeds of my book *From Cabin Boy to Parachute General* and to settle my family (five sons and two daughters). Please give your approval and entrust the execution of this plan to Reichsminister Backe, who knows all about it, as the fulfilment of my last wish.

In the last days of the Third Reich Ultra reported the last grand row among its chiefs. An unsigned message addressed to Himmler on 22 April stated that the writer understood that Hitler could no longer carry on the government and that the occasion had therefore arrived for the writer to take over. The writer was fairly obviously Goering and this was made certain by two facts: signals intelligence was able to say that the message had been sent from Obersalzberg or nearby, and a slightly earlier Ultra message had reported Goering's arrival there. The Reichsmarschall seemed to be distraught. His first step on arrival was to implore Hitler to leave Berlin and come south. He then changed his view and decided that the mantle had fallen on himself, very injudiciously telling Himmler so. Next, having quickly realized his error, he backpedalled furiously in another message to Hitler protesting his undying loyalty, but too late to save himself from arrest. Hitler decided that he had incurred the penalty of death but remitted it out of consideration for his long years of service to nazism and allowed him to resign all his posts on grounds of health. A sheaf of further messages announced that the new number two and Hitler's successor was Grand Admiral Doenitz.

# 5  A VERDICT

BP's achievement was spectacular but not unique. American successes in breaking Japanese cyphers before and during the war have for long been publicly known. Before Pearl Harbor the Americans misapplied and threw away this great advantage, but less than a year later they used it with a vengeance. At the Battle of Midway, which was the American tit-for-tat for Pearl Harbor and the turning point of the war in the Pacific, Admiral Yamamoto was brought to battle and his fleet was virtually destroyed by an opponent who had been reading his most secret messages and knew his dispositions. His ships were sunk while they were still out of sight of the enemy. And yet there was on Admiral Nimitz's side an element of luck which illumines the chanciness of this weapon. The Japanese cyphers which he was reading were due to be replaced at the beginning of April. Owing to problems of distribution the new cyphers did not come into use until the end of May. Midway was fought on 4 June.

American penetration of Japanese cyphers was not without effects in Europe. Although BP was not able to read the secret traffic of the topmost nazi chiefs the Americans, by reading the reports sent to Tokyo by the Japanese ambassador in Berlin, gleaned information about Hitler's plans and his state of mind. The Japanese ambassador and his staff knew the right people and got around. The military attaché, for example, was taken on a tour of German defences in Normandy shortly before the invasion of June 1944. He made a careful report to his ambassador who repeated it to Tokyo and so unwittingly to us. It included detailed measurements, in centimetres, of tank traps and other obstacles on and behind the beaches.

The Germans too had their cryptographic successes. They read French military traffic from 1938 to the French collapse in 1940. In the summer of 1939, just before war began, they broke the cypher used between the War Office in Paris and the regional military HQ in south-eastern France. On the outbreak of war the French extended the use of this cypher to all military

103

regions with the result that the Germans were able at a stroke to read the entire wireless traffic passing between the War Office and its regional HQs.

On their eastern fronts the German listening services intercepted a great deal of Russian talk, broke numerous low-grade cyphers and were able to predict Russian intentions by analysing the comparative volume of signals traffic in different areas at different times.

They broke the cypher used by United States attachés. This was one of their most valuable operational successes, so long as it lasted. The American military attaché in Cairo was fully informed about British dispositions and plans in North Africa and reported them equally fully to Washington. These reports were read in Berlin. They were particularly valuable in the summer of 1942 when Rommel's third offensive won him Bir Hacheim and Tobruk and carried him into Egypt. But just before Montgomery took the offensive in reply the British decyphered an Italian appreciation of the situation which stated that Rommel's successes had been in good measure due to his reading of the American military attaché cypher — whereupon it was swiftly changed and the Germans ceased to read it.

The most successful of the various German decyphering services was the navy's B-Dienst which had begun reading British naval cyphers in 1936. (These were not then machine cyphers, which the navy was slower to adopt than the other services.) The B-Dienst contrived to read operational British traffic within a few weeks of the outbreak of war and was massively successful during the Norwegian campaign. In spite of setbacks in 1940 and 1941 when the Admiralty made changes to make things more difficult for the enemy the B-Dienst was never out of action for long and during 1942 it made a major contribution to the all-important war against the Atlantic and North Sea convoys, producing decodes at the rate of about 2,000 a month. Further security measures on the British side brought about a gradual decline although the B-Dienst, unlike some of its sister services in Germany, never altogether gave up.

The most significant verdict on the German cryptographic services is that most of them gradually stopped trying. British cypher security triumphed in the end (the Germans seem never to have read a high-grade American cypher). One reason was the superior willingness of the British to believe that even their high-grade cyphers might be vulnerable and to act accordingly. The Germans had their qualms about their own cyphers from time to time but they usually managed to stifle them. Early in 1942, for example, Army Group North (on the Russian front) was worrying about the security of some of its orders. At the same time 16 Army, in the same area, issued an instruction that designations in regular use — e.g. O Qu. or Ic (the German abbreviations for quartermaster general and chief intelligence officer) — were to be dropped and a variety of proper names used in their place. A few months later the same army staff was nervously suggesting that a new cypher machine was needed. In January of the next year a high-level conference in Germany announced the introduction of a version of the well-known Hagelin machine, but nothing happened. Later on the Supreme Command of the Armed Forces (OKW) proposed some unification of cypher services and cypher security but it was opposed and baulked by the combined forces of Ribbentrop, Goering and Himmler, all defending their own empires. Finally, in November 1944 Hitler belatedly stepped in and charged the OKW with responsiblity for the security of all cyphers, but it is not clear whether this order was every implemented. A few months earlier a conference on cypher security had recognised Enigma's theoretical imperfections and recommended that Enigma settings be changed after every 70-130 letters; but again the recommendation seems to have been without effect. In the particular case of the reversal of fortune in the Atlantic in 1943 the Germans concluded that their enemies' successes were due to high frequency D/F and improved radar tracking. Elsewhere they were prone to lay any blame that there might be on their Italian allies.

I have already indicated other reasons for the Germans' comparative failure to keep their cyphers inviolate: the faulty operating procedures on Enigma up to the eve of the invasion of France in 1940 which gave BP its first entries into this traffic; mistakes by operators who did not stick rigorously to the rules; the failure to create any equivalent to BP and the consequent dispersal of talent and opportunities among a number of separate and often disharmonious establishments. It has also been conjectured, and it may be the case, that the eviction of the Jews deprived Hitler's Germany of brainpower which could have made a difference.

Then there were too the mentality and the achievements of the blitzkrieg. Hitler started the war. Those whose minds are on aggression are in the nature of things less concerned with intelligence of any kind than are those who inopportunely find themselves with their backs to the wall. At the core of the ethos of nazi Germany was an immensely confident and thrusting arrogance which gave a low priority to intelligence. When the war started German intelligence was in many ways superior to British intelligence but German successes were due less to good intelligence than to the circumstances which obviated the need for it. And as the war went on British intelligence improved wonderfully whereas German intelligence did not.

The early victories of the German armed forces confirmed their imprudent indifference to the co-ordination and organization of intelligence while at the same time creating opportunities for the other side. As the Germans precipitated themselves away from their settled lines of communication, they were forced to throw vast quantities of talk into the air. The first prayer of the cyptographer is for quantity. BP got it. Ironic justice lurks in the fact that the more your operations succeed the more you imperil your most secret communications.

Ultra proved its value in a variety of ways. It could, first of all, be negatively revealing. Here are two examples. In December 1940, six weeks after Mussolini invaded Greece, Wavell attacked the Italians in North Africa. BP was able to read most of the traffic of the Italian air forces in both theatres, but Churchill and his Chiefs of Staff were less concerned about what the Italians were doing than about what the Germans might do. Would Hitler send aircraft or even tanks to Africa? Ultra showed no relevant Luftwaffe moves and since air cover would be vital for the transport of ground forces, this negative evidence satisfied the Chiefs of Staff that for the time being Hitler was not joining the battle in Africa (although he soon did). Without Ultra there could have been no such assurance.[1]

[1]Although the Italians used a version of Enigma in the Spanish civil war, they made only sparing use of machine cyphers in the

A second example: before 'Torch' — the Anglo-American landings in North-West Africa in November 1942 — we were reading relevant German army, air and naval cyphers and we could see that the Germans did not know where the allied armadas were making for. They could hardly have failed to know of their existence, since they comprised nearly 300,000 men with vast quantities of equipment and were making long journeys from American as well as British ports. At the end of September an agent 'with good connections in the Vatican' had reported that there would be major landings between mid-October and mid-November by the Americans in West Africa (Dakar) and the British in North Africa. This was revealed to us in the army Enigma passing between the German army HQ in Rome and Panzer Army Africa. Naval Enigma added its mite. Mediterranean naval Enigma was running at this period at the rate of about 60 decyphered messages a day. Most of this traffic was concerned with the positions of merchant ships at sea and in harbour and their cargoes, but it also included regular reconnaissances of Gibraltar and its Atlantic approaches. So we knew what they knew about conditions in and around Gibraltar and could overhear their speculations. Thus early on 7 November the German naval command in the Mediterranean, reporting the movements of large allied forces, deduced from their size and composition that, apart from supplying Malta, they might be covering considerable landings; but the landing areas named were the Tripoli-Benghazi area, Sardinia and Sicily.

But even more important, both for its extent and its negative conclusions, was Luftwaffe Ultra. From it we could watch the Luftwaffe's defensive build-up in the Mediterranean, its uncertainties about whether a major attack might come at the

second World War. Upon Mussolini's declaration of war in 1940 BP was reading Italian high-grade non-machine cyphers but then lost the army and air traffic temporarily and the naval traffic for good. An exceptional Italian Enigma message from Rhodes contributed to the action of 28 March 1941 off Matapan where the battleship *Vittorio Veneto* was damaged and three other Italian capital ships were sunk. Luftwaffe Enigma also helped to warn Admiral Cunningham that something special was afoot. This action eliminated the Italian surface fleet as a threat to sea-going traffic in the Mediterranean.

western end or in Greece, and observe that no special re-inforcements were being flown to the theatre as D-day appro-ached. This knowledge of the enemy's ignorance and relative passivity was not only reassuring; it was certain. Since by this time we had from Ultra a panoramic knowledge of the German forces, we could tell that units which could be switched were not being switched. We could therefore confidently assert that the failure of additional squadrons to show up in the new theatre was not due to our failure to spot them there but was confirmed by the fact that they were all positively known to be elsewhere. In intelligence the negative can be very positive.

So long as the Germans held the initiative, the question what they might be thinking of doing next was crucially important. Even negative intelligence from a source like Ultra was a boon. For example, was Hitler intending to invade Spain and take Gibraltar? It was valuable to be able to say that we had no signs of such a venture and that if it were to be undertaken — not merely thought about — in the next month or so our source would almost certainly warn us in good time.

Positive intelligence of enemy intentions was, in the nature of things, even more valuable. Ultra's contribution was varied. It commonly gave short-term intentions, e.g. orders for recon-naissance for the next day or days. Intelligence of this kind was used to hamper the reconnaissance aircraft or shoot it down, and to draw deductions about enemy preoccupations and plans. Ultra also provided or helped to reconstruct longer-term intentions. These might change and Ultra might be expected to report the changes. But it did not always do so, and it was always necessary to remember that reading a man's cor-respondence is not the same thing as reading his mind. Rommel's first campaign in Africa was a case in point. Rommel was ordered to attack in May. We knew this from Ultra and we knew that he did not dissent. But privately he determined to attack not in May but in March. At some stage he changed his mind without saying so, and since he did not say so we did not know of the change.

Occasionally Ultra would yield a single self-contained piece of information which was directly and immediately valuable. I remember an incident soon after the invasion of Normandy in 1944 when we were able to give warning of a German parachute operation about to take place behind our lines in the

Cotentin peninsula. It was by no means a large operation but it would have killed a number of people whose lives were saved by the warning. In the same vein but on a larger scale was the revelation, which I described a few pages back, of Rommel's plans at the Mareth line in March 1943.

But this was not Ultra's characteristic style and if I were to single out its most typical contribution I would pick its constant and thorough delineation of the German order of battle. I have already said something about this and I need do no more at this point beyond reiterate the inestimable advantages of knowing day by day where enemy units were; how strong they were; what their supplies of arms, ammunition and fuel were; and, when occasion arose, where they were being told to go. Ultra took the blindfold off our eyes so that we could see the enemy in detail in a way in which he could not see us. This boon, which I have illustrated from Panzer Army Africa, worked even more consistently and fully for the Luftwaffe. Appendix Two gives further examples.

When a few years ago the breaking of Enigma cyphers was disclosed to an astonished and — in Germany at first — incredulous public, one reaction was to say that all histories of the war would have to be re-written. This is not so. In the first place these histories, in performing the historian's basic task of recounting what happended, have told a story which remains fundamentally unaltered. Secondly, even in relation to the questions how and why, many chapters in the history of the war remain unchanged or nearly so. There is no need to rewrite current accounts of such crucial battles as Stalingrad or the Battle of Britain. That, however, is not universally true. In other instances Ultra's role was such that existing accounts are seriously incomplete or misleading.

Two stand out. First, the campaigns in North Africa were materially affected by BP's consistent and prompt breaking of Luftwaffe cyphers and its somewhat spottier and less speedy breaking of German army cyphers. These breaks not only gave British commanders a picture of Rommel's order of battle, his capabilities and shortages; they also enabled the British to put the screw on by intercepting German and Italian supply traffic across the Mediterranean. Whether Rommel would have been defeated if his opponents had not enjoyed these advantages is a question which cannot be answered with certainty. What is certain is that Ultra had a very great influence on the manner and timing of his defeats and on the comparatively light cost to the victors.

The second and strategically much more important instance in which Ultra may claim a decisive role is the war against the U-boats. It is at least possible that without Ultra the Battle of the Atlantic would have been won by Doenitz, and so it becomes possible to speculate whether Germany might have won the war in the west in 1943. Speculate: but no more. A victory for the U-boats, or the prospect of such a victory, could have forced the United States into counter-measures which — because the need did not arise — we can neither divine nor assess.

But an estimate of Ultra's effects on the fortunes of war cannot be confined to particular instances, however vital these episodes may have been. The breaking of the cyphers used by the German army in North Africa and the breaking of the U-boat code in December 1942 were achievements of singular significance. The latter, associated above all with the name of Alan Turing whom even BP's most brilliant cryptographers put in a class of his own, is exceptional both for its strategic consequences and for its technical complexity (the German navy having introduced the extra wheels which made the cryptographer's task the more formidable). But no less remarkable in a different way was the persistent daily breaking of the main Luftwaffe cypher from May 1940 to the very end of the war. Forty years later the mere thought of the range and extent of our knowledge of the Luftwaffe brings one up short. And not the least strange thing about it is how quickly, during the war, one came to take it for granted — just one of those things that happen when you get into a war. But it was none the less extraordinary and, as I have tried to show earlier in this book, our ways into the secrets of the Luftwaffe furnished us with precious information about a variety of other matters too, from the operations of the German army to the scientific secrets of current and projected German weaponry.

This sheer range and volume of intelligence provide the ground for a final factor in the assessment of Ultra's import-ance. Ultra created in senior staffs and at the political summit a state of mind which transformed the taking of decisions. To feel that you know your enemy is a vastly comforting feeling. It grows imperceptibly over time if you regularly and intimately observe his thoughts and ways and habits and actions. Knowledge of this kind makes your own planning less tentative and more assured, less harrowing and more buoyant. Directing a great war is exceedingly tiring. Good intelligence reduces the strains wonderfully. It conditions the two major elements in war-making: the choice between strategies, and the choice between ways of implementing the strategy you have chosen. When, for example, Churchill, Roosevelt and their Chiefs of Staff met at Casablanca in January 1943 to decide what they should do after they had cleared North Africa and recovered control of the Mediterranean, they had been receiving a steadily increasing stream of Ultra intelligence about the enemy for three years. Without it their view of the war would have been entirely different, very much less distinct. With it they still had to take fearfully difficult decisions but they could go about them without having to grope. And they felt they could.

*

On the night of 9-10 July 1943 an allied force of 160,000 men was sailing across the Mediterranean to make landfall in Sicily and conquer it, the first step in the invasion from any quarter of German-occupied Europe. Sicily was defended by nearly half a million Italians and Germans stationed in the island.

In the event the British landings at dawn on the 10th were unopposed and the American almost so. Within a few hours of the first assaults it became certain that 'Husky', as the operation was called, was a complete success.

Yet a few hours earlier, when the approaching convoys were still on their way, this success could not be taken for granted. Landings so audacious had never been attempted before. The preparations had been detailed and protracted. At BP we had been told months in advance that an invasion of this kind was to be undertaken and, with other branches of air intelligence, we had been asked to forecast how many fighter sorties the Luftwaffe would put up over the landing areas on the first day, and for how many days it would be able to maintain this effort. Elaborate and successful deception had forced the Luftwaffe to spread itself over Sardinia and Greece, so imperilling its command of the air over Sicily — a process which Ultra was able to monitor. But the pay-off comes only on the day.

I stayed that night at BP. It remains my most vivid memory of the war, although I had nothing much to do. I caught up with some back reading and wandered round Hut 3 talking to anybody who was not too busy to talk. Like every intelligence officer at some point or other I was temporarily reduced to the role of spectator, waiting for the curtain to go up. But an unusual curtain, because what I was waiting for was the breaking of Red and what this would show me was the German view of the battle. Soon every Luftwaffe unit in the battle zone would be sending into the air not only its aircraft but also its reports on how they were faring and what they were going to do next. Then our circuit would come to life: the intercept stations would be taking down the encyphered German signals and teleprinting them to BP, Hut 6 would be putting them back into German, and Hut 3 would be scanning them for intelligence to send to the allied commanders in charge of this great event. By the time the coaches were depositing the day shift at the gates of BP we should know from the German themselves how the battle was going on their side. Then some of us would go to bed, for the end of the war was only just beginning.

# APPENDIX ONE:
# NOTE ON DOCUMENTS

This note is concerned with documents pertaining to Hut 3. It shows how little of Hut 3's range has so far been lodged in the Public Record Office.

Hut 3's documents may be classified as follows:

1. Enigma decodes received from Hut 6.

   All these decodes, unamended by the Hut 3 Watch, were copied and bound in 'brown books'. They are the corpus of Hut 3's raw material.

   None of this material is in the PRO and it is not clear whether it still exists.

2. Verbatim translations of these decodes.

   These were sent to London by teleprinter or by bag. The greater number were sent by bag. Comments on the texts were frequently appended by the Military or Air Advisers.

   At the time of the writing of this book none of this material was in the PRO, with one exception. Without it it is impossible to assesss the volume of Ultra or its range, and difficult to assess its contribution to the overall picture of the enemy which, through Ultra, was absorbed by intelligence and operations staffs. The exception is the comparatively short series of decodes — 533 messages between 16 September 1942 and 15 May 1945 — which were sent by the Hut 3 Duty Officer to the Chief of the Secret Service and the Directors of Intelligence at the three service departments but were excluded from the regular teleprinted series. Some of these were relayed, on a strictly personal basis, to Commanders-in-Chief in the field.

   Naval material in this category is being made available in full in the PRO.

3. Signals sent to commanders in the field by Hut 3's Military

and Air Advisers on the basis of selected Ultra decodes. Advisers frequently added glosses from earlier Ultra intelligence.

All these signals are being lodged in the PRO. They provide a complete picture of what Ultra gave to commanders when British or American commanders were in the field. At times when there were no such field commanders, and on fronts where these were not British or American (e.g. the Russian fronts), the PRO is almost silent.

There is in the PRO no explanation of the abbreviations which show who got each signal, nor is there any explanation of the conventions used by Hut 3 to distinguish text from comment or the varying degrees of reliability of information which was less then totally certain.

The number of these signals from 18 November 1943 to the end of the war is 51,826. Signals of earlier date had not arrived in the PRO when this book was finished. The number of decyphered Enigma messages from which this intelligence was selected may have been ten times more voluminous.

4. Ultra intelligence appreciations, forecasts and post-mortems.

These were normally prepared for and sent to the War Office or Air Ministry.

None of this material is in the PRO.

5. The card indexes of 3A, 3M and other sections of Hut 3.

These cards were the essence of Hut 3's work and would contribute the most striking visual and intellectual testimony to its operations.

They are not in the PRO and it is not clear whether they still exist.

6. Internal Hut 3 memoranda.

Such memoranda would include guidance on e.g., German

cover names, or standard renderings of German military and technical terms; instructions on the preparation and despatch of intelligence for commands; and many other topics of prime interest.

None of this material is in the PRO.

7. Memoranda and correspondence concerning the functions of Hut 3; its relations with Hut 6, with other sections of BP and with authorities further afield; security; the advent and integration of the US contingent; and a great deal more which, probably, I never saw and have certainly forgotten.

None of this material is in the PRO.

The PRO contains no material whatever from Hut 6 or its naval equivalent, Hut 8. The only material from the Naval Section at BP is the verbatim translations of naval Enigma decodes teleprinted to the Admiralty (see para. 2 above).

There is no diplomatic Enigma in the PRO nor any hint that there will be.

# APPENDIX TWO:
# STRENGTH RETURNS
# BY GERMAN UNITS

Since the verbatim translations of decyphered army and Luftwaffe Enigma have not been deposited in the Public Record Office this crucial and characteristic form of Ultra intelligence cannot be reproduced here. But there are in the PRO copies of the signals sent by Hut 3 to commands on the basis of these decodes. I append a few examples in order to illustrate the nature, scope and variety of this aspect of Ultra.

The first examples come from the Luftwaffe. The largest operational unit in the Luftwaffe was the Geschwader, which was divided into three or sometimes four Gruppen, which were divided into three or four Staffeln. A Staffel consisted of ten aircraft and the normal operational complement of Gruppe and Geschwader was 36 and 120 aircraft respectively.

A fighter Geschwader was designated Jagdgeschwader, followed by an indetifying number: thus Jagdgeschwader 53, or JG 53 for short. Its Gruppen (JGr) were called I, II, III and IV JG 53. The Staffeln making up these Gruppen were numbered in arabic numerals.

Other Geschwader had different designations: Kampfgeschwader or KG for bombers, Stukageschwader or SG for dive bombers, Nachtjagdgeschwader or NJG for night fighters, etc. Each Geschwader and Gruppe had a small head-quarters unit commonly referred to as its Stab (staff); it included the commander's own aircraft and was operational. A Gruppe would normally occupy a single airfield with its associated Gruppen on nearby airfields, although this pattern became increasingly disrupted as the war went on. A Geschwader might even have its Gruppen on widely separated fronts.

The following examples show something of what Ultra was telling us in June-July 1944 about (a) the strengths of Luftwaffe units, (b) their movements and (c) the occupation of airfields.

*

Second Gruppe J 53 strength on 22nd: aircraft 30 and 8, crews 52 and 22.

J 27 for 23rd: Stab aircraft 5 and 1, crews 5 and 5
first Gruppe 13 and 6, 13 and 13
third Gruppe 15 and 12, 16 and 16
fourth Gruppe 20 and 6, 21 and 17

This signal was despatched by Hut 3 to various British and American commands in France at 2248 hours on 23 June 1944, two and a half weeks after the allied landings in Normandy. Some of the information was for the end of the previous day and some for the day before that. The locations of these units were all known. They were in fact all on the western front. The return is in very abbreviated form but the meaning of the figures had been unravelled for certain. In this case the two figures for aircraft gave the unit's total number of machines on the airfield followed by the number serviceable when the report was drawn up. The figures relating to crews indicated the number of pilots present followed by the number who were operational or, as the Germans said, ready.

Messages of this kind were daily intelligence provender. Here is another, also from the western front, a month later. It was despatched at 1721 hours on 21 July:

A. Stab J 27 return evening 19th:
Stab 2 and 1, 19 and 19
first Gruppe 41 and 30, 52 and 28
fourth Gruppe 25 and 16, 39 and 18
thereof in operational area Angers:
Stab 2 and 1, 4 and 4
first Gruppe 41 and 30, 40 and 8
fourth Gruppe 25 and 16, 27 and 11
(comment: difference gives almost exactly figures for rear element in XL 2821).

B. Stab J 1 return evening 19th:
Stab 3 and 2, 2 and 2
first Gruppe J 5 34 and 24, 16 and 11
third Gruppe J 1 aircraft unknown pilots 52 and 34
losses included one of third Gruppe J 1 missing. 12 aircraft of first Gruppe J 5 ready for handing over of which one unserviceable

C. Return evening 18th ...

122

The last part of this signal gave similar information about a third group of units which were unnamed in the German original but could be identified with certainty by Hut 3 because one damaged aircraft was described in terms identical with another report in the same cypher and because the figures corresponded closely with those in yet another return. The reference at the end of part A to XL 2821 is to a previous signal from Hut 3. The missing information in part B was mostly likely lost through a failure in interception at this point.

*

Operational orders and transfers of units were equally interesting. At 0559 hours on 20 July Hut 3 passed on these orders issued a few hours earlier. A Jagdkorps was a staff controlling a number of fighter squadrons:

> Jagdkorps II order for 20th at 1730 19th: ten minute readiness from 0330 hours. For all units except J 27 area of operations Lion sur Mer — Epron — Britteville sur Laize — Cheville with main effort penetration area south-east of Caen. Mortar Gruppen to be made ready. Operation only on express order. J 27 area of operations Balleroy — Airel — Marigny — Torigny sur Vire.

A somewhat different kind of order, passed on by Hut 3 two and a half hours later:

> Order morning 19th by Jagdkorps II. With immediate effect Geschwader and first Gruppe J 11 withdrawn from operations … aircraft to be given up to first and second Gruppe J 1 …

This order included directions about where the personnel of the withdrawn units were to go. Before the end of the day this destination was switched from one place in western Germany to another.

*

Another kind of Luftwaffe return gave dispositions on airfields. These divided the aircraft into categories which, as the following signal shows, 3A had unravelled. This signal

giving dispositions at the end of the day on 18 and 17
September 1944 was despatched by Hut 3 at 2232 hours on the
19th. I reproduce only the first part of it:

> Some airfield occupations. Comment: first figure total
> aircraft, second in workshops and hangars, third on landing
> area, fourth (where given) in blast bays.
> A. On 18th. Zwischenahn 20, 5, 1, 14
>    Nordholz 23, 2, 0, 21
>    Ludwigslust 123, 34, 0, 89
>    Varrelbusch 6, 0, 6
>    Varel 20, 2, 0, 18
>    Ahlhorn unchanged
>    Grossenbrode 48, 4, 40
>    Stade 29, 17, 5, 7
>    Neustadt Glewe 17, 0, 17
>    Wesermuende 23, 18, 3, 2
>    Hagenow 101, 16, 64, 21
>    (strong indications Marx) 28, 3, 0, 25
>    Hoernum 5 BV 138 of which 4 unserviceable
>    3 Dornier and 11 Cant Z 506
>
> B. On 17th ...

The aircraft at Hoernum were seaplanes. It was of some
interest to note two days later that at Ludwigslust, the most
populous of these airfields, the total of 123 had sunk to 87. The
figures for Grossenbrode do not add up, probably a slip by
whoever compiled the return.

\*

Similar returns from ground units ranged from the very simple
to the very complex. Here to begin with is a simple one. It is a
manpower return for a division. When relayed by Hut 3 it was
five days old.

> Return on 18 by 12 SS Panzer Division. A 413, 1900,
> 14674 B 86, 351, 2477 C 499, 2251 17151 and 208
> voluntary assistants. Suggest on previous evidence A equals
> fighting troops B equals commissariat C equals total.

A second example from army traffic shows how very much

124

more complicated this intelligence could be. It is a report on the state of affairs in a Jaeger (Light) division. A Jaeger division comprised two Jaeger and one motorized artillery regiments and four specialized battalions. The message is incomplete. The first part is missing. Presumably it was not intercepted. Furthermore, the message presented a puzzle because it introduced two new categories into what had been a simpler routine form. And something has clearly gone wrong at the German end with paragraph III 19.

Hut 3's signal was despatched to three allied headquarters in the Mediterranean theatre at 2316 hours on 24 June 1944. Owing to the loss of the first part the deciphered message itself does not give the date for which the return is valid but the time of interception would make this clear enough. Comment supplied by Hut 3 is in brackets.

Report of state of 42 Jaeger Division. (Comment: beginning not available. Pro forma includes new headings C and D meaning of which not known but A and B still seem to represent strength and deficiency. Figures in order A B and then C D if present.)

II Personnel
    3. Men 10855, nil
    4. Voluntary assistants 173, 1848

III Material
    1. Pistols 2734, nil
    2. Rifles 11 773, nil
       Rifles 41 352, 115, 177, nil
       Telescopic sight rifles 168, 32
    3. MP 428, 580, 40, nil
    4. LMG 511, nil
    6. 8 cm. or 12 cm. mortars 104, nil
    7. LIG 13, 2
    8. SIG nil, 4, 4, nil
    9. LFH 9, nil
    10. SFH 7, 1, 1, nil
    12. Heavy A/T guns 22, nil
    13. M/C 54 of which 34 not fit for the field, 140, 161, 12
    14. Cars 52 of which 27 not fit for the field, 132, 171, 5
    15. Lorries 100 109, 275, 233, 47
    16. Eastern tractors 18, 23

17. Semi-tracked tractors 1 ton  nil, 23, 31, nil
18. Ditto 3 tons  unspecified of which 8 not fit for the field, 1, 1, nil
19. Ditto 8 tons  3754, 875 (comment: not known whether figures or interpretation incorrect)

List exclusive of motorized infantry and heavy infantry gun platoons of Jaeger regiments 25 and 40, former still being in Germany.

IV        State of training: varies. Some elements still lack basic training and weapon and firing training especially on the very large number of captured weapons, also specialist training. Training as a formation for the most part completely lacking. Employment of division in coast defence makes training difficult. Training being pressed forward, instructor detachment of C-in-C South West weapons school being attached for purpose.

V        Special difficulties: serious deficiency motor transport makes difficult supply and supervision of troops employed over wide area. Owing lack supports for medium loads with artillery Abteilungen [sc. detachments] guns cannot be loaded on mules but moved only in tandem.

VI        Operational readiness: conditionally ready for defence.

This detailed account of the not very happy situation in a comparatively static division may be contrasted with intelligence of a different kind from a different zone of operations. On the same day, 24 June 1944, Hut 3 was reading a series of messages about reinforcements for the German armies in France. Here are two signals sent, with priority ZZZZ, at 0605 and 1020 hours on that day:

Of II SS Panzer Corps and 9 SS Panzer Division 27 trains had arrived in area C-in-C West by 18th, of which 21 trains arrived Nancy. Information 21st. Of II SS Panzer Corps

STRENGTH RETURNS BY GERMAN UNITS

and 9 SS Panzer Division 78 trains in area C-in-C West of which 62 unloaded area Nancy, 10 (slight indications Dreux) and west of Paris. Elements of corps arrived in assembly area Laigle — Nogent — Le Rotrou — Alencon. Of 10 SS Panzer Division 62 trains in area C-in-C West of which 47 trains unloaded area Saarbruecken–Nancy, 15 in area Dreux and west of Paris …

The signal continues with details of this kind unit by unit and concludes … 'Further details follow.'

The first reference in this signal to Dreux illustrates one of Hut 3's rules. It is all but certain from the further reference to 'Dreux and west of Paris' a few lines further-down that '(slight indications Dreux) and west of Paris' really is Dreux. But if the German text was not crystal-clear the Hut 3 officer was not allowed to give the name unqualified. Probably what happened was that the British interceptor missed the word Dreux, so that when the text reached BP it showed that the name of the place in question had five letters, all or most of which were wrong or missing. If the decyphered text had been less corrupt but still not clear, the Hut 3 officer might have written 'fair indications Dreux' or 'strong indications Dreux'. However sure he was of the interpretation, he could not say simply Dreux if that word did not stand clearly in the German text.

# INDEX